Introduction to Bharata's Nāṭyaśāstra

Bharata's *Nāṭyaśāstra*, the earliest treatise on dramatics, is, even today, the origin of our dramatic tradition. Besides being the most important study of dramatics, it is also the most comprehensive. The all-inclusive quality, however, creates problems for the reader who has to go through a great deal of unnecessary information. In his *Introduction to Bharata's Nāṭyaśāstra*, the author has culled all information essential and relevant to drama, eliminating the superfluous. Eschewing attempts to provide any kind of a scholarly or original interpretation of Bharata's views, the author has focused on giving the reader a connected account of the study of dramatics using modern terminology. The purpose is to introduce those interested in drama to Bharata's wisdom and to throw light on the state of dramatics in ancient India. Written in a simple and lucid style, the author takes the reader through topics like theatre houses, the stage and stagecraft, play-construction and the *rasa* theory. All lovers of drama are sure to find this book both useful and absorbing.

Adya Rangacharya (1904–84), was born in Agarkhed, district Bijapur. He has his education at Bombay and London universities. His writings were original and prolific, which made him a trend-setter among Kannada and Indian writers. His works include twelve novels and a number of scholarly book on the theatre, on Sanskrit drama and the *Bhagavadgītā*; but it was as a dramatist that he made his mark (47 full-length and 68 one-act plays).

His other works in English are: *Drama in Sanskrit Literature; Indian Theatre; The Nāṭyaśāstra*, English translation with Critical Notes; and *Introduction to the Comparative Philology and Indo-Aryan Languages.*

Introduction to Bharata's Nāṭyaśāstra

Adya Rangacharya

Munshiram Manoharlal
Publishers Pvt. Ltd.

ISBN 978-81-215-0829-2
Second reprint 2011
Reprinted 2005
First published 1966

PRINTED IN INDIA
Published by Vikram Jain *for*
Munshiram Manoharlal Publishers Pvt. Ltd.
PO Box 5715, 54 Rani Jhansi Road, New Delhi 110 055, INDIA

www.mrmlbooks.com

Contents

Preface to the Second Edition

Shri Adya Rangacharya, one of the most eminent authorities on the *Nāṭyaśāstra*, was one of those who combined both scholarship and creativity to an almost equal degree. His reputation as a dramatist has, however, tended to overshadow his scholarly work on the theatre, on Sanskrit drama in particular. This book, an *Introduction to Bharata's Nāṭyaśāstra*, was perhaps a kind of stepping stone to the more massive task of translating the entire *Nāṭyaśāstra*, which was one of the last tasks he undertook, translating it both into Kannada and English. However, as he himself says, since the *Nāṭyaśāstra*, contains all the available information on the various arts, the contemporary reader could get lost in that bewildering maze. In this book, he has therefore culled all that is relevant to drama only and rendered it in contemporary terms, making it easily accessible to any reader today. For a student, enthusiast, scholar or performer of drama it is of course ideal—all the more so when one considers how little material there is really on the subject.

This book, first published in 1966, has been out of print for some time. I am very glad that Munshiram Manoharlal Publishers are reprinting it and making it available once again, fulfilling a need much felt in dramatic studies.

SHARADA ADYA RANGACHARYA

Bangalore
May 21, 1997

Preface to the First Edition

In preparing this short book I am fully conscious both of my limitations and my advantages. I may speak here frankly about the former and leave the latter to be detected by my readers.

What I intended to do here was really work for a number of scholars working in a group over a number of years. I am only one and I am impatient. Even after Independence I found no signs of any University or any Akademi (Central or State) recognising the importance of research work on *Nāṭyaśāstra*, leave alone thinking or providing for it. On the other hand, a foreign Professor of Dramatics in a Foreign University (have we any such professors in our universities? how many?) once highly recommended to me Bharata's wisdom. As an Indian I felt proud, as a Sanskrit scholar I felt sorry that this sincere foreigner was apparently misguided by some cultural delegation type of Indian scholar. My reaction to what I felt then is these few pages.

For twenty years I was a Professor of Sanskrit and University teacher for Ancient Indian Culture; for more than thirty years I have been writing dramas. Here I have tried to avoid the special weakness of both. I am not pedantic nor am I fanciful in my interpretation of Bharata. Even if anyone accuses me of either 'offence', I would feel happy in the hope that my 'offence' would provoke either a younger or a more hard working scholar to improve on my attempt. For the merits, if any, in this book the credit would go to my wife Smt. Sharada Adya who was prompting me so insistently to write whatever I felt about the *Nāṭyaśāstra* that I finally decided to say my lines lest the prompting be heard by the audience. Secondly, Shri Sadanand Bhatkal of Popular Prakashan, Bombay, has a claim on my gratitude for he agreed to publish this book without even asking about its contents. I hope to deserve his trust.

ADYA RANGACHARYA

1

Introduction

Nāṭyaśāstra, a treatise on drama and dramatics and allied subjects, is attributed to one Bharata or Bharatamuni as he is called more often in our tradition. The usual trappings of a *muni* (sage) are nowhere mentioned; on the other hand, his sons satirised the sages and the latter, enraged, cursed them to be turned themselves and their descendants, into śūdras (XXXVI, 29-35). Though Bharata is honoured as the first writer on dramatics, nothing is known about him or the time he lived in or any other such personal details. The word 'Bharata' is the name of the son of the famous king Duṣyanta (hero of Kālidāsa's play); the word also means 'an actor'; and it is doubtful whether as applied to the author of *Nāṭyaśāstra* it is a proper noun or a class noun. Even a cursory reading of the text would show that this is the work neither of one man nor of one time; as a matter of fact, if Bharata were an authority on drama, here in this book other subjects like music and dancing are given so much importance, that it is strange the book is called *Nāṭyaśāstra.* On the other hand, it seems as if someone later on tried to bring in one volume all the available information on the various arts. Actually, it is the boast of the book that there is no knowledge, no craft, no lore, no art, no technique and no activity that you do not find in *Nāṭyaśāstra* (I, 116).

The work, in the form in which it is available today, consists of thirty-seven chapters; the usual style is the metrical one, but also prose in a number of places (particularly in the chapters on *rasa, bhāva* and also on music). The total number of verses is 5569. In addition to music and dance, the subjects dealt with are semantics, morphology, the various dialects and their phonology, play-writing, play-construction, production, rehearsal, acting, dramatic criticism, drama-audience, producer and many allied crafts. There are references to other writers and other views; there are unnecessary repetitions, there are contradictory passages, there are words the technical meaning of which tradition has no trace; in one work, all the elements that could make a book difficult to an average reader are there. A drama gives knowledge *(vibodha)* to the ignorant *(abodha)*, says the author (I, 110); as written earlier it was a huge volume, says Bharata, and takes credit for the present volume which, he says, is both short and simple. Perhaps, Bharata addressed these words to his contemporaries since an average modern Indian would hardly find it simple. So what Bharata did for his contemporaries, this present book proposes to do for the twentieth century Indians (and all others interested in the subject); for this reason, there would be no attempt here to know who Bharata was, whether there was an actual Bharata, what time he lived in, whether the present work is entirely his or from time to time his school followers added and padded, whether, etc. Whatever the answer to those questions, the importance of the work would not be affected nor its wisdom detracted; on the other hand, the influence of Bharata on the rural stage up to the modern days and throughout India (irrespective of the difference in languages) compels us to accept the book on the whole in its present form. The present work is not a scholarly thesis nor an original interpretation. It is no more than a rendering in modern terms and technology all the information (concerning drama only) contained in the *Nāṭyaśāstra.* Here and there the present author has attempted to supply the connecting thought (as scholars do the missing words in the manuscript); otherwise, as could be seen throughout from references to the text, it is mainly the story that is narrated by Bharata and the views he expresses on the different aspects of the study of dramatics and the production of plays.

2

Origin and Objectives

The *Nāṭyaśāstra* begins with the description of how drama originated. In the Indian tradition there is no difficulty in tracing the source of anything and everything. The explanation is very simple. The Trinity of Brahmā, Viṣṇu and Rudra (or Śiva) manages the world by a sort of division of labour; thus Brahmā creates, Viṣṇu nourishes and Śiva destroys. Since all the three represent omnipotent Godhood the question as to why the three Gods continue this repetitive game does not arise. God Brahmā creates everything and so he created drama also; the only point worth remembering is that unlike the material world drama was created on a special requisition of the smaller gods. It happened thus:

Once, a long time ago, during the transitional period between two Ages it so happened that people took to uncivilised ways, were ruled by lust and greed, behaved in angry and jealous ways with each other and not only gods but demons, evil spirits, *yakṣas* and such like others swarmed over the earth. Seeing this plight, Indra and other gods approached God Brahmā and requested him to give the people a toy *(krīḍanīyaka)*, but one which could not only be seen but heard and this should turn out a diversion (so that people gave up their bad ways) (I, 8-11).

But apparently Brahmā did not feel flattered by this request. After all he had created all beings and he had also created the Vedas to give them knowledge for a better way of life. If people took to bad ways it meant that they were neglecting or ignoring the Vedas, the sacred lore in which was contained all knowledge. But Indra explained that it was not so; of course, the Vedas were there and many people were benefited by them. But, unfortunately, the śūdras were prohibited from learning, nay even from listening to the Vedas (I, 12). In the circumstances, the remedy lay in creating another, a fifth Veda which would be accessible to all the four castes (I, 12).

Thus, it was Indra who by his diplomatic skill induced God Brahmā to create a *Nātyaveda*; for this contribution of his, Indra, as we find later, was given the honour of inaugurating the first ever play. However, to proceed with the story, Brahmā created a treatise as requested. It seems that the book dictated by this God of four faces (and tongues) turned out not only tough but voluminous. Indra took the book with him, read it to other gods and then came to the conclusion that the gods were unable to understand, digest and put into practice the contents of this book. "They are incapable of any dramatic activity" is how Indra put it to the Grand Old God (I, 22). Probably these gods were used to an easy life; study, hard work or intellectual activity of any sort was unknown to them. So Indra finally proposed to Brahmā that a search for a proper person be made among the sages since they were studious and hard-working (I, 23). Thus, it was that the final choice fell on Bharata, who was asked to take charge of the work. Naturally, Bharata abridged the voluminous work so that it could be used by the mortals; secondly, he was asked to produce a play. "You have got hundred sons and, therefore, you be the producer," said Brahmā to Bharata (I, 24). It was easy, particularly in those good old days, for a father to maintain strict discipline among his sons. "I got the *Nāṭya-veda* from God Brahmā and started teaching my sons and also rehearsing them," says Bharata, suggesting cleverly that next to God Brahmā he is the originator of our drama.

To what extent does the foregoing narration help us to understand the origin of drama? Do we accept the fanciful divine origin? or should we say that the narration is in the terms of those days when men accepted the leadership of gods and the only way to establish an idea was to say that it originated from god himself? Though Bharata or the author whoever he was seems, from one point of view, modest enough not to take the credit as the first one in the field, from another point of view, he hints to us that his views are too divine in origin to be debated and that he himself was selected by the Great God himself as the only capable or qualified one. If we look at this narration carefully, we do feel that Bharata is not undeserving of his boast. Whether before Bharata there was or there was not any drama, the drama which he gives is one that definitely was not there. The words describing the circumstances that compelled Indra to approach Brahmā are very significant (I, 8-12).

1. "uncivilised (or vulgar) standards (*grāmya dharma*)"
2. "people were swayed by lust, greed, anger, jealousy, etc."
3. "a toy (plaything) is desired"
4. "create a fifth Veda accessible to all the castes"

In these phrases we find the views of Bharata on drama, its nature and its objectives. Bharata, as we feel, does not and has no intention to describe the origin of drama as such; on the other hand, he describes how his views on drama came to be formed compelling him to formulate rules about it. It is apparent that even before him there was drama but that was given to *grāmya dharma* (uncivilised ways), that described elemental passions like anger, jealousy, lust, greed, etc.; in other words the drama that was there was not 'a Veda', i.e., knowledge-giver; it was a drama of, by and for people to whom knowledge was denied. Indra is very particular in saying to Brahmā that "another, a fifth Veda, accessible to all the castes" be created. He does not ask for drama as such but adds that this fifth Veda should be a diversion (an entertainment) to both eyes and ears. Probably, before Bharata, there was no *nāṭaka* as defined by him. The stage-shows were called *rūpaka* and hundreds of these have been recognised by Bharata himself. Most of these dealt with low *śṛṅgāra* or low humour. Bharata apparently resolved, in the name of the gods, to improve the public taste. But he knew that he could not do anything that would affect the popularity of drama. So he particularly described a *krīḍanīya*—an entertaining toy. On the one hand, it was entertainment *(krīḍanīya)* and, on the other, an enlightenment (Veda). These two characteristics were insisted upon by Bharata and the result was what we now call the urban theatre or a sophisticated drama. Bharata is the originator of this Theatre and this Drama.

The story as narrated in the first chapter of *Nāṭyaśāstra* corroborates such an interpretation as the forgoing one. Bharata, in obedience to God Brahmā, accepted the task and started coaching his sons. Words, movements and actions (the three *vṛttis*) were also rehearsed; at this stage, Brahmā suggested that dance and music (*kaiśikī vṛtti*) be also introduced. Bharata agreed to one condition, viz., that females should volunteer to play since "it was impossible for males to express female sentiments, etc." Brahmā created *apsaras* women (I, 45-46). Finally, when the rehearsals were complete (I, 53) Bharata got ready for performance on a day which luckily was Indra's festival day (I, 54). The show, however, was not destined to be a success. Since the story showed the defeat of the demons by the gods, the former led by Virūpākṣa decided to prevent it and finally disturbances broke out; demons were routed but the play could not be performed. The demons decided to repeat their obstruction for any second show (I, 78); so, Bharata had to seek protection from Brahmā who ordered the heavenly architect Maya to construct a theatre-house and a stage. Before putting the show in this theatre-house Brahmā called a meeting of gods and demons and explained to both of them the nature of a play; it is not any propaganda so that whoever, is depicted in an uncomplimentary light need no feel hurt; it is impartial in its outlook so that anyone and everyone may come in either for praise or ridicule; its object is first to entertain and then to instruct, so it must be taken in that spirit. "A play shows your actions and emotions. Neither gods nor demons are depicted as always good or always evil. (Actually) the ways of the world are represented here. It gives you good advice, it gives you enlightenment and also entertainment. It provides peace of mind to those who are afflicted with miseries, sorrow, grief or fatigue" (I, 106-7, 112-14). Bharata, at least, does not seem to have been troubled any further by the demons.

Two or three things in this part of the story deserves to be noticed. To begin with, Bharata feels that a theatre-house is a necessity. Of course, the circumstances in which he conveys that necessity is an extreme example. That disturbances are likely to be created is one of the reason; there are other reasons which are even more important and we shall notice them in due course. But a theatre is a necessity as well for the audience as for the actors and Bharata gets it sanctioned from Brahmā.

Secondly; the participation of lady-artists. In some portions of the *Nāṭyaśāstra* there are hints and mild suggestions that women should not be given any roles (XXVI, 10-11). But it is clear from the first chapter and some other contexts that Bharata's view was that some roles were done better by women than by men, and particularly gestures, motions and emotions of women could be properly conveyed by women only (I, 46).

Thirdly, the nature and purpose of a drama, according to Bharata, are emphasised here. The play proposed by Bharata "is an insult to us and complimentary to gods" said the demons (I, 103). But God Brahmā tells them that no drama should be looked at from a personal or narrow point of view because there is represented not any particular individual but generalised observation of the world and its ways. No motive either should be attributed to the dramatist because his intention is to give good advice through entertainment (I, 107). The element of entertainment is emphasised more than once. However, it is an entertainment that does not excite you, on the other hand, that brings you peace of mind (I, 114).

This is the story of the origin of Drama in the form which Bharata gave it. Just as Pāṇini standardised classical form of Sanskrit, so Bharata standardised classical form of drama. He gave it status and dignity, a form and an objective and finally a technique. It is immaterial whether Bharata was an actual individual or when he lived, etc. Like Aristotle among the Greeks, Bharata in India stands as one of the greatest law-givers for good taste in literature and drama. *Nāṭyaśāstra* is a work codifying those laws. If Bharata actually lived then on his death his disciples might have shouted "Bharata is dead, long live Bharata"; for the present *Nāṭyaśāstra* seems to convey the views more of a school of thought over a period of differences and debates than of any one individual.

3

The First Production

As we have seen above the first production was in need of a good deal of publicity. God Brahmā wanted gods and demons to have a proper perspective. "Do not be angry with the gods," he advised the demons, " because drama, as visualised by me is only imitation" (I, 117). As a matter of fact "The entire behaviour and activities of the people in their joy and sorrow is represented here through gestures and movements." (I, 119).

After establishing a peaceful atmosphere, the Grandfather God suggested a procedure which would further bring gods and demons together and make them forget their grievances. This was the worship of the stage that had been put up by the heavenly architect. It is an elaborate procedure and it should be understood only in the context of the social and religious life of those days. Beginning with the lathi (*jarjar*) which beat down the demons when they first created disturbances and including the various deities, every nook and corner of the stage is worshipped. "Never put up a show without worshipping the stage; these (gods and demons) respect you when you show respect to them, they worship you in return for your worship for them," says Brahmā (III, 98). It is not surprising, in view of our tradition, that till today *raṅga-pūjā* (worship of the stage) is done before the curtain goes up.

A whole chapter (III) is devoted to the description of this worship. Though one can understand our tradition to think of such a ritual, one would hardly expect a whole chapter of 102 verses to be devoted to it. Is it the worship of the stage or of the various deities and spirits that are supposed to "possess" the different nooks and corners of the stage? In the text itself there is a sort of confusion and a lot of unnecessary repetition.

1. "This worship of the deities of the stage is equal to a sacrifice." (III, 97).
   "This is the procedure of worshipping the deities of the stage." (III, 102).
2. "One who puts on a show without worshipping the stage." (III, 98).
   "The producer should worship the stage in an undisturbed frame of mind." (III, 101).

In the two passages above and the contiguity of the verses concerned one could see the clumsiness of the text.

Moreover, in an earlier context (in chapter one to be exact) God Brahmā has already blessed Bharata and asked him to put up the show. There is no reference to all this elaborate ritual.

"This indeed is a good occasion. This is the festival of Indra." (I, 54).

With this blessing of the great God Himself, Bharata set about his first production and then the demons created all the rowdyism. The idea of having a theatre-house naturally arose out of this experience and the next chapter describes the various types of theatre-houses. It should be noted that the particular theatre-house required by Bharata has been built in the first chapter itself, and Brahmā in company of gods and others went to see it; it was approved and finally Brahmā instructed the gods to look well after it (I, 79-83). This also makes the elaborate worship a second thought. We would rather suspect a later writer to interpolate this long ritualism than expect God Brahmā's blessings and instructions to be ignored. Even in the first chapter from verse 83 to the end there is clumsy mixture of two contexts, one defining the nature of drama and the other elaborating the stage-worship. Though the last verse of chapter I mentions *raṅga-pūjā* (stage-worship) the beginning of chapter II ignores it and the question put there to Bharata is "Would you tell us about the theatre-house because that is the first thing (requisite) in the context of a dramatic performance?" (II, 3). And finally, chapter IV begins (except line 1 of the first verse) with Bharata asking Brahmā what play to put on the stage. This question comes naturally after chapter II. The first line of the first verse of chapter IV refers to stage worship and what follows shows that this is a poor and clumsy justification of one whole interpolated chapter.

The first performance of a play (not the earlier attempt foiled by the demons) as described at the beginning of chapter IV should be treated like the great, historical event it must have been. Here was the first performance of a play written by Brahmā himself and produced by a learned sage (IV, 3) and witnessed by gods and demons—i.e., a mixed crowd of gentlemen and others. Till now, the educated and the cultured had no stage for themselves; the popular stage was too popular to be literature or a prophylactic of taste. Even otherwise it was of a type more likely to turn into or lead to a rough house. But now here was stage which "gods and demons" could watch together and derive benefit from, while the earlier one was such that "gods" could not join the usual crowd of "demons". So, the first production of Bharata was a special occasion. From the beginning intelligent planning had gone into the production. "All my hundred sons were there, each in an assigned role, and each in a role to which he was quite fitted." (I, 40). Bharata speaks of his preparation. He had acquainted himself with and seen other performances; "Why, I have also seen a play in *kaiśikī* style, expressing the sentiment of love, in which God Śiva himself was dancing", he says (1, 45). Reference to the sentiment of love, *śṛṅgāra rasa,* is significant. We shall see later that the various types of popular plays (*upa-rūpakas*) contained either low *śṛṅgāra* and low *hāsya* (comedy).

Like a research scholar collecting his materials, Bharata had witnessed all kinds of shows. With confidence in his ability, experience and observation he trained his sons for the play called *Amṛta-manthana.* The episode of churning (*manthana*) the ocean for nectar *(amṛta)* ends in victory of gods against the demons. Now we can understand why the demons had taken objection to the play. But since the play was written by the very god who creates laws also, there was no chance of its being censored or prohibited. Brahmā himself admits, though indirectly, that it is a propaganda play when he says "put that play on the stage; it will enthuse and please the gods" (IV, 2). In the meanwhile, the eloquence of God Brahmā's four tongues must have mellowed the demons and (or) Bharata himself must have been a great producer because seeing the play "both gods and demons, all of them, were pleased" (IV, 4). The play showed in imitation the actions and the emotions (*karma* and *bhāva*) of both gods and demons (who, in the original episode, had churned the ocean). In producing the play, Bharata had not projected his own preferences or prejudices towards the characters, hence, there was nothing to resent.

The play *Amṛta-manthana* is mentioned as a *samavakāra* which is one of the ten forms of stage-shows recognised by Bharata. Almost all the writers on dramatics have accepted as a historical fact that *Amṛta-manthana* was the first play and that, in form, it is a *samavakāra*. One cannot be sure of the historicity, but that is immaterial. However, tradition seems to be so strong regarding Bharata's first produced play and its type that even in a critical study it has to be accepted for whatever its value. We shall see later what a *samavakāra* form is like. For the present, it is enough to remember that a *samavakāra* is the first play produced by Bharata.

4

Theatre-House and the Stage

We have seen earlier how Bharata came to feel the necessity of a theatre-house. Before we proceed to study his views on theatre-house, it is better we clarify one or two things. Bharata uses words like (1) *nāṭyaveśma, nāṭya-gṛha, nāṭya-maṇḍapa;* (2) *raṅga-śālā, raṅga-bhūmi, raṅga-maṇḍapa;* (3) *prekṣya-gṛha.* Word in group (1) are used to denote an entire play-house; in group (2) *raṅga-bhūmi* would mean the stage, while *raṅga-śālā* or *raṅga-maṇḍapa* would mean like *prekṣya-gṛha* just an auditorium.

In the beginning of chapter II the sages ask Bharata details about the theatre-house which is mentioned in the previous chapter as having been built by Maya. The sages preface their question by adding that "a theatre-house is the first requisite of a dramatic performance" (II, 3).

The description of the theatre-house as found in chapter II is repetitive, conflicting and confusing. To begin with, Bharata says that three shapes (*sanniveśa*) of a theatre-house have been fixed by Viśvakarman (the heavenly architect), namely, (1) *Vikṛṣṭa* or long-drawn out, (2) *Caturasra,* square or all round, and (3) *Tryasra* or triangular (II, 8). Further it is said that sizes also are fixed as three, viz., *jyeṣṭha* or big, *madhyama* or medium and *kanīyas* or small (II, 9). Now, the point is if each of the above three shapes could be in one of the three sizes in which case we shall have nine varieties in all. That at least seems to be the meaning or the suggestion of II, 9 and 10 in which Bharata says:

"Of the three (shapes) are three sizes, big, medium and small. The difference is in the measures of *hasta* and *daṇḍa*. (24 fingers = 1 *hasta*; 4 *hastas* = 1 *daṇḍa*." (II, 8).

"108 *hastas,* 64 *hastas* and 32 *hastas* (are the three measures); 108 is the big size, 64 the medium and 32 the small." (II, 10).

In these three measures one could have three shapes of each measure—in which case *vikṛṣṭa* would mean simply 'big', and not necessarily 'long drawn out' when the sense conveyed would be that the length would be greater than the width. The three types of *vikṛṣṭa* in three measures, would be as follows:

	Size	*Length*	*Width*
1.	*Jyeṣṭha*	108	64
2.	*Madhyama*	108	32
3.	*Kanīyas*	64	32

Similarly, three *caturasras* would mean three squares of the respective sides of 108, 64 and 32 measures. If, however, *caturasra* means 'all-round' and not a square then the three *caturasra* sizes would be

Size	*Length*	*Width*
Big	108	108
Medium	64	64
Small	32	32

Finally, the *tryasra* would be three equilateral triangles of sides 108, 64 and 32 respectively.

Now in the same context a few verses later we find the following passages:

Tryasra is considered to be the small one, *caturasra* the medium one and *vikṛṣṭa* the big; this is the opinion of expert producers (II, 14b-15).

This verse, however, instead of clarifying the confusion adds one more uncertainty. We have three measures as big (108), medium (64) and small (32), and we have also three names corresponding to the size as *vikṛṣṭa, caturasra* and *tryasra*. But we learn nothing about the shape of the theatre-house. If *vikṛṣṭa* is the big one and 108 is the measure for the big size, would a *vikṛṣṭa* theatre-house be 108 × 108, or 108 × 64 or 108 × 32? It must be one and one only from these three since according to this view there are only three types in all. Similarly, would *caturasra* be only 64 × 64 (because it must be medium-sized) and *tryasra* only an equilateral triangle of size 32? It is not clear. The only general ideas we get about the theatre-house, forgetting the confusion about their shapes and sizes, are two:

1. "The theatre-house for gods should be the big one, that for kings the medium one and for others the small one" (II, 11b-12a).

   At first glance this seems to be another effort on the part of a third or fourth interpolator to avoid the conflicting meanings of verses discussed above. Whatever the shape and whatever the size, the thing that should matter is that big, medium and small must go respectively with gods, kings and others. But as we find even with the earlier commentator Abhinavagupta, the meaning of this verse is something more than is conveyed by the words. It is not that gods in heaven would have a big theatre, kings in palaces a medium and others a small one. This is not the meaning. The description here is from the point of view of the theme or story of the play. If the story deals with gods (and demons, etc.) then, according to Bharata, the stage must be big, since the number of characters, the actions, the movements, etc., do require plenty of space; if with kings and their love and life story then a medium-sized theatre would do; finally with the story of common men a small stage would suit the occasion. The idea of the size of the stage depending on the type of the story is an important one from the point of view of the success and the effectiveness of the production.

2. The second general idea is contained in five verses in the same chapter:

   "The theatre-house, for the mortal beings, may be 64 measures in length and 32 in width; it need not be larger than this" (II, 20b-21).

   "Because, (if larger), the play would be (seen and heard) indistinct; with a big auditorium characters have to shout their lines and in that distance they may not be heard at all; similarly, the facial gestures, etc. would not be clear; speech and songs should be clearly heard; for this reason, a medium-sized theatre only is preferred." (II, 22-26).

   The inconveniences of a small theatre seem to be implied according to commentators; in a small theatre, the speeches, etc. would sound loud and the facial gestures would look artificial.

   The theatre-house, according to Bharata, must fulfil two conditions: (1) it must have a stage which in dimensions would suit the story and (2) it must have an auditorium from which the words and acting would be clear and look natural.

The text of the *Nāṭyaśāstra* describing the construction of a theatre-house is very corrupt and even Abhinavagupta is in great difficulties when commenting/referring to the construction of a theatre-house in *Nāṭyaśāstra.* Side by side with his own interpretation he also mentions other views and other interpretations. Modern scholars too are not agreed among themselves and each has his own interpretation. Though this situation would justify the propagation of another view, it would not be advisable in the interests of trying to get Bharata's, and not any other, views.

We have seen above the two main conditions which Bharata expects a theatre-house to fulfil. Let us try to understand his description of a theatre-house in the light of those conditions. Before doing so, it is necessary to remember that a theatre-house, according to Bharata, could not be a permanently built structure; because day-light was the main light on which the producer of those days depended, the theatre-house would not be one that would be walled on all sides and roofed from above. At the same time protection from the elements of Nature had to be provided and to that extent, a sort of top covering both for the stage and the auditorium could be expected.

In II, 20 and 21, as we have seen above, Bharata has preferred, for the mortal world (and beings), a theatre-house 64 measures in length and 32 measures in width. He has also said that this is the *madhyama* size in addition to being the most convenient size. Though this would be the average size of a theatre-house, other sizes could not be precluded since Bharata himself suggests changes according to the story of the play. But, as he is greatly in favour of this medium size, we may take that in case of stories involving "gods and demons", etc., the length shall remain 64 measures, but in view of a bigger stage being required, the width also may be 64 instead of the average 32 measures. Similarly, when a small stage is required, suitable adjustments may be made with the average measure of 64 × 32.

How is such a theatre-house constructed? Bharata starts from the very beginning (II, 29ff). The producers, he says, must first examine the site which should be "level, firm, hard, black or white soil". Then it should be cleared of all rubbish (like bones, skeletons, etc.) and shrubbery and then measurement laid out. A number of ritual ceremonies, superstitious omens, etc., are then mentioned. After scrupulously observing all those, a plot 64 × 32 measures should be laid out. The length of 64 should be divided into two halves. Now we have one 32 × 32 and another 32 × 32; of these two one would be for the auditorium and the other for stage purposes. In this context a number of words are used in the *Nāṭyaśāstra* and, as is to be expected there is no consistency about their meanings; probably, later interpolations used them without knowing the distinction of the earlier days. For example we have (1) *prekṣya-gṛha,* (2) *nāṭyaveśma,* (3) *nāṭya-maṇḍapa,* (4) *raṅga-bhūmi,* (5) *raṅga-maṇḍapa* and so on. These words do not mean one and the same thing; the first one would mean an auditorium, second a theatre-house, third a drama auditorium, fourth a state and the fifth again an auditorium. Many passages could be understood, many contradictions explained if we understand the words as above. Now, to go back to the description of a theatre-house, we can now say that one-half (32 × 32) would be used as stage (*raṅga-bhūmi*) and the other half (32 × 32) as the auditorium (*raṅga-maṇḍapa*). On the stage Bharata describes three sections, (1) *raṅga-pīṭha,* (2) *raṅga-śīrṣa,* and (3) *nepathya-gṛha.* Later in the chapter Bharata refers once again to the three shapes (1) oblong (*vikṛṣṭa*), (2) square (*caturasra*), and (3) triangular (*tryasra*).

Here does one find confusion worse confounded; even Abhinavagupta is not sure of the meanings and side by side with his own alternatives he refers to others' views. He hints at different readings. In one word, intuition and luck more than scholarship are likely to help us here.

Raṅga-pīṭha as we can understand is the front portion of the stage and it may be broadly understood to be equivalent of our present stage-front. In the stage portion of 32 × 32 *raṅga-pīṭha* measures 8 × 32, i.e., lengthwise one-fourth ot the stage-area is *raṅga-pīṭha*; behind this another portion, 8 × 32, is called the *raṅga-śīrṣa,* head of the stage; finally, the remaining portion, 16 × 32, is called *nepathya-gṛha* (comprising green-room, costume-room, etc.). This seems to be too simple to be believed and, as we read other passages, we find we cannot believe it—unless we understand or bear in mind the significance of the different shapes of a theatre-house. The above description seems to apply only to the oblong one. The *raṅga-śīrṣa* in this oblong house is to be higher in level (II, 106) than the *raṅga-pīṭha* so that actors in deep scenes are more clearly visible. But the *nepathya-gṛha* behind that would be on the same level as the *raṅga-pīṭha,* conveniently under neath the *raṅga-śīrṣa,* so that direct entry, under special circumstances, is possible from the *nepathya-gṛha* to the *raṅga-pīṭha.* In the case of *caturasra* and *tryasra* the *raṅga-pīṭha* could be a *vedikā* (raised platform) (II, 104) while *raṅga-śīrṣa* and the *pīṭha* are on the same level, one behind the other. If so, what about the sight being obscured? But here, we have to read and re-read passages and put two and two together to deserve a clear reply to this question. For example, in II, 93 it is said that for a *caturasra* the measure should be 32 all round *(samantataḥ)*; and, again in II, 108, speaking of the stage in a *tryasra* theatre-house, Bharata says that it should be a triangle within a triangle. Now putting these two together we can arrive at the following (justifiable) conclusions:

1. Unlike as in the case of the oblong theatre-house, the stage (half in area as in *vikṛṣṭa*) was, in the case of the square and the triangular houses, a square and an inner triangle within the bigger square and the bigger triangle.
2. In both these cases *raṅga-śīrṣa, raṅga-pīṭha* and *nepathya-gṛha* were on the same level; but
3. one-half of the inset square and the lower trapezium of the triangle with two sides bisected formed both the *śīrṣa* and the *pīṭha* with the *nepathya-gṛha* running along both and doors from the latter to enter into the two former.

Finally, one feature may be noticed in the case of both the square and the triangular houses; viz., in both these the audience could be all round the stage.

So far we have only tried to understand about the stage itself. But in Bharata's view, the auditorium, too is equally important since he wants it to be such that all that is shown an all that is said on the stage is clear to the audience. In II, 87, the author says:

> The *nāṭya-maṇḍapa* (auditorium) should be in the shape of a hillock or a cave and of two levels (*dvi-bhūmi*), with lattices or small windows, without any strong breeze and one where the voice is loudly carried.

In spite of the way we have translated it, the verse, in the original, has been the cause of a number of interpretations, none of them clear. The word responsible for this uncertainty is *dvi-bhūmi.* Abhinavagupta, after mentioning a number of others' views, ends with his own preceptor's view according to which *dvi-bhūmi* is interpreted as rows of rising seats as in a gallery. The sense has to be forced out of it.

In this connection it should be noted that before the stage is prepared, Bharata speaks of two things, (1) the erection of pillars and (2) the erection of four *maṭṭavāraṇīs.* Now, by observing the traditional method of creating a stage—we can straightway say that the *maṭṭavāraṇīs* are four elephants with raised trunks which are the corner supports of the stage and then we have four pillars in-between. In other words, the stage is a *raised* platform. In the case of a *vikṛṣṭa* house there shall be eight supports on which a platform is put up. In the case of a *caturasra* (II, 96-97), since the stage is in the centre, there are ten supports and the *raṅga-pīṭha* is in the form of stairs (that is rising steps). In this case, the seating of the audience (II, 98) would be on ground level on which (all round) rising stairs (one *hasta* steep) would be arranged; the same applied to the auditorium in a *tryasra* house. The arrangement of the auditorium and of the seating differs according to the different type of theatre-houses. In all cases the two levels—that of the stage and that of the auditorium—are different (*dvi-bhūmi*). [Even nowadays touring companies set up an auditorium and a stage in a simple way. They dig up a particular area a foot deep, and this area the auditorium; the earth that is dug up is neatly heaped along this auditorium (usually one foot high) and this raised level is the stage. Here also the sense of the phrase *dvi-bhūmi* can be understood.]

This, then, is the *lakṣaṇa* or 'definition' (II, 3) of a play-house which Bharata gave to the sages who were eager to hear from him all about drama and dramatics.

5

Pūrvaraṅga

The foregoing discussion of the building of theatre-houses is the subject-matter of chapter II of the *Nāṭyaśāstra.* We have already seen how the topics of worshipping the stage and its deities described so elaborately in chapter III seems to be out of context. After the construction of a theatre-house, Bharata is asked to produce a play called *Amṛta-manthana* (IV, 3). Seeing their actions and emotions so well represented on the stage the gods and the demons were greatly pleased (IV, 4). After sometime Brahmā suggested to Bharata that a play be shown to God Śiva (IV, 5) and they went to him and finally showed him a play called *Tripura-dāha* (IV, 10). The audience was greatly pleased and so was God Śiva who incidentally said that from his own experience of dancing he thought dancing could be used with good effect during the *pūrvaraṅga* (IV, 14). Till now, *pūrvaraṅga* was nothing more than the preliminaries like welcoming the audiences, describing the story or tuning or drumming instruments. But God Śiva suggested that instead or in addition of dance with appropriate music could be introduced. Bharata agreed.

This *pūrvaraṅga* has, in the course of time, become an elaborate ritual. But originally it was, as a later writer (Śubhaṅkara by name) puts it, just *sabhāpūjā*—worship (or respectful welcome) of the audience. It is called *pūrvaraṅga* because it comes before (*pūrva*) the performance (*raṅga-prayoga*) (V, 7). Originally, it began with playing on drums and instruments (as is done now hours before a *yakṣagāna* performance is due to begin). Bharata has a common sense explanation for this. He says that instruments that could arouse interest and curiosity should be played upon since the auditorium would be consisting of "women, children and foolish persons" also. In other words, the original purpose of *pūrvaraṅga* was to keep audience curious and interested about the play to begin.

The suggestions of God Śiva turned out very useful since dance and music could keep the audience interested. So in chapter IV Bharata, in acceptance of Śiva's suggestion, describes elaborately dance and music that could be utilised in the *pūrvaraṅga*. Earlier, Śiva asks Taṇḍu to demonstrate and this demonstration, known as Tāṇḍava, is also described. The description is so elaborate that it runs from verses 19 to 266. This rather confuses Bharata's audience. "We can understand about acting which conveys definite meaning. But this dance and this music seem to have no meaning. What use are they?" the sages ask Bharata (IV, 267-68). Bharata agrees that there is no meaning as such attached to dance but "since it adds beauty to the occasion people naturally like it. And also it is considered as auspicious and entertaining, so you have it during marriages or on happy occasions."

As said earlier even in the *Nāṭyaśāstra* (IV, 269-71), the *pūrvaraṅga* is described with a number of details; but the underlying idea, in spite of various attempts to make it an elaborate ritual, is to invoke the protection of gods, etc., and the interest of the audience. So, in the same context in which details are profusely (and even fancifully) described, the *Nāṭyaśāstra* has the following observations:

Thus you have two varieties of *pūrvaraṅga,* one pure (*śuddha*) and the other mixed (*citra*); but, regarding dance and music one should not ever do it. When there is too much music and dance and playing on instruments, not only the actors but even the spectators will be tired (or bored). An audience that is tired would not enjoy *rasa* and all the following performance may not interest it. (V, 162-64).

Actually the *pūrvaraṅga* was developed to serve another useful purpose. Though originally it was what the actors and the *sūtradhāra* did before the performance began, with experience it was found useful to extend it into a prologue to the play. So the 'behind-the-curtain' part of it ended with the invoking by *sūtradhāra* blessing of gods to both the audience and the actors. This was called the Nandī, unnecessarily explained etymologically as one which pleases the gods. Probably, the origin of the word in this context is different. Nandī was also a character like Taṇḍu who belonged to the tribe led by Śiva. Since *pūrvaraṅga* was revised as suggested by Śiva, Taṇḍu's dance and also Nandī's music were included in it. It is not merely something that pleases the gods because actually it is supposed to put even the actors and the audience into a pleasing mood.

So with Nandī by *sūtradhāra* one part of the *pūrvaraṅga* is over; now the play begins but before that some preliminaries are found necessary, and so *pūrvaraṅga* may be considered to continue even after the 'curtain-rise'. The immediately preceding item is the Nāndī and this Nāndī according to the *Nāṭyaśāstra* (V, 107-12), "invokes gods, wishes well to the twice-born, proclaims loyalty and victory to the ruling king, hopes prosperity to the kingdom and fulfilment of the ambition of the stage, wishes *dharma* to the spectator and fame (or success) to the author, and all the time the two accompanying actors would be saying 'amen'."

From the above description we find that nothing is left out by way of good wishes or thanksgiving; but all this would take place unseen by the audience. Now when the play begins, it might be said as if the curtain rises even while this is going on; because, the first thing done as soon as the play begins is to invoke blessings similar to the above. Curiously enough, as soon as the play opens, the *sūtradhāra* ceases to be *sūtradhāra* and is called *sthāpaka* (one who introduces); naturally, he is described as having the same figure and features as *sūtradhāra* because it is one and the same person. This *sthāpaka*, after welcoming the audience with god's blessings introduces the occasion. This was done in the old days since plays were not performed but only on special occasions; sometimes it is a festival of a god, sometimes it is joyful occasion (like when an heir is born to or victory is won by the king, etc.), sometimes it is simply because the leading citizens have expressed a desire to see the play and so on. After explaining the particular occasion, according to the type of the play, the audience is entertained for a short time by a dance or a song (by the female character *naṭī*) or the audience is given all necessary information about the play and the story or sometimes the story itself is introduced through some clever literary device and so on. Often times, the season of the year was theme of the song. The reason for this was that a play was performed not only among beautiful surroundings but mostly during day-time. Thus, in chapter IV, when Bharata gave a special show for Śiva and his followers, the site he selected was "on the slopes of Himalaya, surrounded by hills and summits, full of mango trees and with brooks running in the valleys" (IV, 9). Later in chapter XXVII (verses 80-85), he gives the time of the day when a play should be performed:

That which is pleasing to the ears and deals with the praise of good behaviour should be performed in the first part of the day;

That which deals with noble characters, full of sounds (and music?) and full with noble or heroic deeds should be performed during the afternoons;

A play in *kaiśikī* style, with music and dance and orchestra and dealing with a love-story (lit. erotic sentiment) should be performed in the evening.

One which deals with greatness of character, with pathos as the main sentiment, should be performed in the early morning (lit. dawn), such a play drives sleep away;

A play should not be performed at noon or midnight nor during the twilight hours or dinner time.

The time of the day probably gave the audience an idea about the type of the play and it was the duty of the *sthāpaka* to take the audience into his confidence. With the passing of time this part of the *pūrvaraṅga* came to be known as *prastāvanā*. As a matter of fact dramatists were not at all particular about the details of the *pūrvaraṅga* or the characteristics or name of the prologue. In many plays *sūtradhāra* continues to be called as *sūtradhāra* and not as *sthāpaka*; the *prastāvanā* (prologue), according to the characters involved or the style of introduction, came to be known as *viśkambhaka* also. But the underlying sense of a *pūrvaraṅga*, viz., to keep the audience interested, curious and informed did not continue with all good dramatists. So it is time that the play begins.

6

Abhinaya

I

With the backing and help and approval of Gods Brahmā and Śiva, Bharata has already developed from a producer into an authority on dramatics. That is why sages have crowded round him asking questions and listening intently to Bharata's replies. Now after Bharata has described the *pūrvaraṅga*, the immediate question the sages ask is "give us a reply to five questions". In some interpretations, the reference to 'five' is taken to mean the five questions asked in chapter I where the sages desire to know, which are (1) the origin of drama, (2) the purpose of drama, (3) the divisions and classifications, (4) the authorities, and (5) the nature of a dramatic performance. But after the *pūrvaraṅga* in chapter V, the next chapter opens with this request for a reply to 'five questions'—and, as it happens, five questions do follow, viz.: (1) what is a *rasa*, (2) what is a *bhāva*, (3) what is a *saṁgraha*, (4) what is a *kārikā*, and (5) what is meant by *nirukta*. All these five questions are answered in chapters VI and VII. If, however, we go back to the five questions of chapter I, it would be hard to justify the place of a discussion of the *rasa* theory after *pūrvaraṅga*. In the first five chapters we are still trying to understand the 'birth' of drama; the story is not complete, so chapters VI and VII discussing *rasa, bhāva,* etc., seem to be out of context here. After *pūrvaraṅga* the play begins, in other words the play is performed on the stage and this performance is the medium through which what is conveyed by the play is understood by the audience. The performance is thus the 'technique' (= artistic mode of expression as the dictionaries put it). The performance, i.e., the technique covers actors, their words, their movements, their gestures and so on as well as the actual stage with its connotations. Naturally, this topic should come next. Therefore, leaving out the consideration of chapters VI and VII for the present, we go to chapter VIII which begins with the question, what is *abhinaya*?

The word *abhinaya* is usually translated as 'acting' but as it is used in the *Nāṭyaśāstra* it has a very wide meaning, a meaning that includes not only what we understand by 'acting' but other things which go to make up the medium of expression. In answer to the question to the sages Bharata explains (VIII) the word etymologically from the root *nī* to carry, with the preposition *abhi* meaning 'towards'; that which carries the meaning (lit. the performance) to the audience is called *abhinaya*. And this, adds Bharata, is of four kinds, *āṅgika, vācika, āhārya,* and *sāttvika* (VIII, 9) (of these the first one, *āṅgika,* is described in six chapters beginning with chapter VIII). What does *āṅgika* mean? That which is derived from (or due to) the *aṅga,* i.e., the body. "Bodily acting would include many modes from simple gestures to deliberate postures and artistic movements. The untiring thoroughness of Bharata could be clearly seen in these six chapters. First of all, he tells us that 'bodily acting' should be seen under three heads: (1) physical gestures (due to body or *śarīra*), (2) facial expressions (from different parts of the face), and (3) postures or movements (*ceṣṭā*). Under the first head, Bharata mentions six 'main limbs' (*aṅga*) of the body, viz., hands, head, chest, sides (or hips), waist and feet; the facial expressions are conveyed by eyes, eyebrows, nose, lips, cheeks, and chin; these six are called *upāṅgas,* i.e., 'subordinate or secondary limbs'. An example of each of these would give an idea of the kind of bodily acting. In the case of the 'head' the author mentions thirteen kinds of movements, each conveying a meaning, e.g., there is a variety called *adhogata,* i.e., downcast. The "downcast head conveys the sense of bashfulness, salutation and also grief" (VIII, 34). What is interesting is the kind of *obiter dictum* at the end of describing all the thirteen varieties. "Of course, there are many other ways (of conveying meaning by the position and the movement of the head) but those can be studied by observing the habits of people and then introduced into the acting" (VIII, 36). Similarly in the case of 'eyes', the author describes thirty-six kinds of glances conveying thirty-six different meanings. In all these cases, what he describes is neither the definition nor the prescription for acting. As the author himself says time and again, in a drama you have a representation of actions and emotions and since there would be as many ways of expressing these as there are individuals, there could be no hard and fast rule nor a uniform mode of expression on the stage. Nevertheless, since the main purpose is to convey the sense to the audience, the modes must be such as would be known to the audience with their meaning. It should not be understood that these gestures and modes are studied by the actors and to that extent mechanical. Bharata insists that in all these cases, as in ordinary life so with the actor on the stage, the gestures and the modes must be accompanied by the look on the face (*mukha-rāga*).

Bodily gestures, etc., if unaccompanied by facial expressions do not convey any charm or attraction, physical gestures even if inadequate, will be twice effective if accompanied by facial expression, "like the moon during the night time" (VIII, 162-63). Without facial expression, other "bodily acting" would be as dull as the moon during the day-time. So chapters VIII and IX describe in detail the nature and the meaning and the varieties of the acting of six *aṅgas* and six *upāṅgas.*

In the next chapter is described what is called a *cārī*. The meaning of this word seems to be a 'pose'. In the first verse of this chapter—the verse itself being considered as an interpolation—a *cārī* is defined as a pose which brings in a line waist, hips, thighs and feet. A *cārī* is not a movement and also not a gesture which comes naturally like nodding the head. It is a deliberate stance. The author of the *Nāṭyaśāstra* says that "except by a *cārī* there shall be no movement in a play" (X, 6). Throughout chapter X, a number of poses have been described which represent actions of different kinds. Examples like one shooting an arrow or riding a chariot or holding the reins of the horses, etc., illustrate what is meant by *cārī.* In all such poses the author tells us that hands, feet, hips and waist must be in line with the action suggested (X, 45-56). What the author wants to convey is that on the stage one's movements should be not only deliberate but artistic. As everyone from the auditorium is watching the actor, he has to stand, turn, move about, etc., in a manner in which the spectator feels pleased and interested. Therefore, *cārī* or poses—stylised movements—are prescribed both *bhaumya* i.e., belonging to or treading on the earth or *ākāśikī* in the air, i.e., to convey running, jumping, etc.

If *cārī* is a pose then *maṇḍala* described in chapter XI is movement resulting from a number of *cārīs* (XI, 1). In representing fights, battles and such incidents involving movements *maṇḍalas* are to be employed (XI, 63), if necessary, to the accompaniment of musical instruments.

Chapter XII describes a different kind of actions and movements and the subject-matter of the chapter is called *gati-pracār,* i.e., gaits and movements; e.g., we are told how to walk when we are feeling cold, how to glance when we are fleeing from some terror, to walk as a merchant or as a king would walk, etc.

"With quick steps one must show the moving of a chariot, with bow and arrow the warrior in the chariot...or with face up, as if you are flying into the skies, with face down as if you are descending to the earth, etc." (XII, 82-85).

Here also the author ends by saying that there is no hard or fast rule but you observe people and their behaviour under particular circumstances and enact likewise—though these were not listed or described here (XII, 119).

Thus, under the heading of 'bodily acting' we have (1) the movements of the *aṅgas* and the *upāṅgas,* (2) the *cāṛīs,* the *maṇḍalas,* and (4) finally the gaits or movements under given circumstances. The 'bodily acting' is the first of the four kinds of acting.

II

The next is *vācika,* i.e., lit. belonging to speech. But just as in the case of 'bodily acting' what was described was what we now call body-control, so under *vācika* the subject is more what we consider as voice-control and less concerning speaking or language. Unfortunately, the relevant and irrelevant are so mixed up that in the four chapters (XIV-XVII) supposedly dealing with this topic we have other topics like phonetics, prosody, metres and figures of speech, etc., and it is only the last chapter that is more relevant to the context.

In chapter XIV starting with vowels and consonants, the author goes on to describe the formation of words, and then the various parts of speech. In the next chapter we are told about how words go to form different metres, the scanning of the various metres follows. Chapter XVI speaks of figures of speech. In all these chapters there are profuse illustrations and sometimes references to other's views. It is only in chapter XVII that the author turns to what may be called 'dramatic speech'—which is neither prose, nor poetry, nor follows the rules of grammar. It actually represents spoken language to begin with, so the author rightly says that in a drama speech language is of four varieties; and it varies according to the social standing of the character on the one hand and the part of the country to which that character belongs. Thus there is the (1) *atibhāṣa*, the grandiloquent language of gods and supermen, (2) the *āryabhāṣa*, the refined speech of kings (and aristocracy), (3) the *jātibhāṣa* or the mother-tongue of ordinary individuals, and (4) the *mlecchabhāṣa* or the corrupt language of the foreigners (and the low-born). In addition, there could be the language of birds and beasts (i.e., imitation of the sounds emitted by them, and this language could have a meaning only in a drama) (XVII, 25-29). It is possible there could be other kinds of dialects not mentioned here but necessitated by the dramatic context (XVII, 62).

In addition, there are some special uses of language, particularly in a drama. For example, the way in which characters address each other; this itself does convey to the audience the status and the mutual relation of the character (XVII, 64). The author painstakingly lists these words.

Thirdly, though in common or everyday life, language is mostly employed for conversation between two actual persons, in a drama it may be necessary for a character to speak to a person who is not on the stage or to converse with a character not on the stage and so on. In such cases intonation is most important. So (XVII, 107-9) the author quotes verses which he calls *ānuvaṁśya*, i.e., handed down by tradition and which describe the nature of *kāku* intonation. Similarly, certain vowels and some consonants, given a special intonation, convey a particular emotion. Even a pause would be significant in a dramatic speech (XVII, 120-26). And then the peculiarities of the intonations of men and women may also have to be studied. Since all these intonations have to be produced deliberately by the actor, this *vācikābhinaya* may rightly be called 'voice-control'.

III

Āhārya, the third kind of *abhinaya,* is simply defined as that which is produced through *nepathya* (I, 2). Now the word *nepathya* also is not easy to understand. It is usual to associate the *nepathya-gṛha* with the 'green-room' and, thus, broadly understand the word, in the sense of 'make-up'. But it should be understood that make-up as understood by the word *nepathya* includes painting and other make-up like beard and moustache as well as costumes and ornaments and everything else that goes to give us the character in the play. Bharata himself explain *nepathya* as of four kinds, viz., *pusṭa, alaṁkāra, aṅgaracanā* and *sañjīva.* Of these, the first, viz. *pusṭa* is explained as follows:

1. Things like mountains or chariots or aeroplanes, etc., that are made from cloth or leather, etc., to be used in a play are called *pusṭas* (XXI, 9).
2. *alaṁkāra* includes garlands, necklaces, ornaments worn on different parts of the body and dress (XXI, 10).
3. *aṅgaracanā* is painting the face and body, and
4. *sañjīva,* according to XXI, 151, is the entry of animals, bipeds and quadrupeds and those without feet, on the stage. These animals should carry (or even be in the form of different kinds of battle-weapons (XXI, 154).

Finally, the author recognises different varieties in each of these. For example, the *puṣṭa* is supposed to be of three varieties (XXI, 6):

(1) *saṁdhima,* i.e., where the mountains and cars, etc., are made of cloth or leather, (2) *vyājima,* i.e., the kind that are made by some kind of mechanical device, and (3) *ceṣṭimā,* meaning where these are shown by means of gestures.

Now, we are in a position to understand what is meant by *āhārya abhinaya.* It includes painting, make-up, costume, property required by the characters (e.g., snake by God Śiva, *cakra* by God Kṛṣṇa, etc.) and the ornaments worn on the body. Throughout chapter XXI the *Nāṭyaśāstra* describes laboriously these things as applicable to characters male, female, impotents (in the harem), young, old, child, rich, poor, beggar, forester, ascetic, king, commander and so on, and so on.

Whether it is this or that character, the *Nāṭyaśāstra* evolves certain general principles applicable to all (and for all times, too).

In XXI, 15, speaking of ornaments the author says, "the variety in ornaments is greatly based on the difference between men and women, between region and region and between caste and caste."

In other words, the ornaments are worn not to make the characters look beautiful or attractive but look genuine in the context of the story and the play. This applies not only to a character but even to an object. Any material in the actual world, when introduced in a play, must be represented with all its characteristics (XXI, 101). Not only that, for the sake of sustaining the illusion that the object is real it should be made in proper proportion (XXI, 155).

For example, the characters in a drama are usually painted not only to lose their previous individuality but also to look the character they are playing. Should the painting of face and body be governed primarily by considerations of the art of painting or of aesthetics or of the drama? As a matter of fact all these would be there though the last one is most predominant. The art of painting will have its say as far as paint and its mixture are concerned; similarly, the sense of aesthetics sees to it that the final result does not produce, in the audience, a reaction prejudicial to the purpose and place of that character in the play. But the considerations of the drama itself must come first and the paint should make the character look not just beautiful and attractive but real in the context. So Bharata says (XXI, 87) that while making-up (painting) the characters one should know "the process about (preparing and mixing) paints, about its lasting quality and fastness and also the region, the caste (family-heritage) and the age of the character (to be played)."

It is very important that outside considerations like region and tradition of the character are taken into consideration, particularly where dressing a character is in question. "A dress that is foreign to the region to which the character belongs would make the character laughable (lit., does not lend beauty)" (XXI, 71). The *Nāṭyaśāstra* describes elaborately proper dresses for male and female characters not only according to the part of the country and age of the character but also according to the status (social) of the character; even different locales would mean a change in dress. What is true of dress or costume is also true of the facial make-up. The southerners should be made up as 'non-white' (*asīta*), the easterners as 'darkish' (*śāma*) and the northerners as 'white' (*gowra*); a forester would be made-up black, and so on. The elaborate varieties listed in the chapter make us admire Bharata for his meticulous and patient observation and bold application.

Lastly, Bharata describes what he calls *pusṭa.* This would mean all that is required by character (in addition to costumes and ornaments) as distinctive of its individuality. This includes masks, weapons, totems and such other things that go and are naturally associated with a character (as a mace with Bhīma or a bow and arrow with Arjuna in *Mahābhārata,* e.g.). Bharata wants us to bear in mind two things about such stage objects:

(1) It is not possible to reproduce them exactly as they are in actual life though it is necessary to make them look outwardly extremely similar to the original, (2) secondly, they should be made of such material that on the stage it would be easy to wield and carry them. They may be prepared from hollow bamboos and cloth but never from iron or any heavy material. Even objects like mountains, mansions, temples, idols, etc., may be made out of lacquer or cloth or hollow bamboos or leather, etc. Such objects must be light (*laghu*) and not heavy (*guru*) (XXI, 190-97). As for weapons they are not meant for actual use like breaking or beating, etc., but are intended to be used symbolically (XXI, 212).

Thus, make-up, costume, ornaments and accessories of characters all together are, according to Bharata, *āhārya abhinaya.*

Though the author has mentioned *sāttvika* as the fourth variety of *abhinaya* we find later on in chapter XXII this being mentioned as *sāmānya.* In XXII, 1, he explains that *sāmānya* is nothing else but what comes as a result of the *sattva,* i.e., essence of the first two, viz., *āṅgika* and *vācika abhinaya.* Thus, the word *sāmānya* is used as a synonym of *sāttvika* and we can take it that the fourth variety is called *sāmānya* or *sāttvika.* It is very difficult to understand what Bharata means by *sattva*; looking to the long list of examples, the word might as well mean grace or charm. What the author means by *sāttvika abhinaya* seems to be expression in a graceful or charming manner the various *bhāvas,* i.e., feelings. Grace or charm excludes improper looks, gestures and movements. That is why the author says,

> Sleeping (or beds) should not be shown on the stage; the sense may be conveyed in some way by words; kissing, embracing and such other things, and eating or water-sport or such other shameful actions are not to be shown either. After all, in the auditorium, there may be sitting (a family consisting of) father, son, daughter-in-law, mother-in-law, etc., and, therefore, such scenes should be scrupulously avoided (XXII, 284-88).

At the same time neither love-scenes nor battle-scenes as such are to be avoided. That is why grace, charm and propriety are insisted upon. The entire chapter goes on prescribing a way of proper acting for scenes and situations involving love and grief. It may be that what is done on the stage is not done in actual life. But still for the sake of charm or propriety instead of representing what is done in actual life the actor should convey the sense in a charming and proper style. Movements and gestures in given circumstances can be said to be stylized here. The variation, if any, comes in because of three types of men and women 'high, low and middle-class' (XXIV, 1). The *sattva* or the grace comes both in speaking and in gestures and movements. These latter should, in addition to conveying the meaning, also lend charm to the mode of expression. The author has further standardized some characters so that for a particular type of character a particular stylized acting could be prescribed. Feelings too are finally analysed so that both the physical and the emotional reactions could be standardized and acting them stylized, e.g., in XXIV the heroes are classified not only by their character and temperament as four kinds *dhīroddhata, dhīra-lalita, dhīrodātta* and *dhīrapraśānta,* but even by the fact of their having one or more wives or loving particular one as against another one and so on. Similarly, heroines are classified not merely on their own merits but even according to the behaviour of the hero towards them; the acting of all these is prescribed under given circumstances. Since these qualities or characteristics are called *sattva* or *sāttvika* quality, the acting that expresses them is called *sāttvika.* The elaborate rules and standardization is mostly about plays dealing with a love story. The reason is obvious. It is here that propriety and decency are likely to be disturbed and Bharata is very particular as already referred to above.

It is interesting to note one point which Bharata discusses; it also shows the amount of common sense and thinking the author of the *Nāṭyaśāstra* has brought to bear on his book. In chapter XXIV, 74-78, he refers to a reasonable doubt. How can any actor express the qualities of a king when he has not sufficient equipment? For example, suppose his dress, his make-up, his costumes, his surroundings on the stage are not the proper ones. How could the actor feel, move or behave like a king? But, says Bharata, even while writing about the requirements of drama. I have provided a satisfaction to such doubts. Why should it be difficult when so many precautions are taken to help the actor forget his identity and merge his individuality into that of a king? He is painted in such a manner that his person is almost concealed; he is decked with suitable ornaments and costumes. All he has to do is to walk in dignified steps, talk in dignified tones, etc. A clever director (*ācārya*) will also see while selecting the actor for such a role that physically too his appearance is appealing or impressive. Therefore, there should be no difficulty.

Finally, the author describes what he calls *citra-abhinaya.* Apparently, this is not a recognised variety since it is not mentioned in connection with the four, viz., *āṅgika, vācika, āhārya* and *sāttvika.* The description of this kind of acting in XXV seems to suggest that miscellaneous rules and directions regarding acting are here collected under the head, *citra.* But in (XXV, 1) he mentions particularly that *citra-abhinaya* is that which expresses, by means of gestures and looks etc., that which is 'not mentioned', e.g.,

1. Expressing thrill (i.e., hair standing on end) one should act the touch to the body or to the mind of things soft or sweet-natured (XXV, 9).
2. By acting avoiding touch or repulsion one should express the presence of harsh or undesirable things (XXV, 10).
3. With body trembling with fear and eyes closed, one should convey the sense of lightening striking or of a deafening sound or of a fire emitting sparks (XXV, 15).

In other words,

"The behaviour of the people is of various kinds; conveying that by acting and bodily movements is called drama (acting)" (XXV, 125).

Bharata finally leaves it to the talent of actors and confesses "it is not possible to form rules (or give directions) for acting or conveying the (unbelievable) various actions and objects of the world" (XXV, 128).

The final authority is the world itself; this should be realised by those who produce and enact dramas (XXV, 129).

7

Stagecraft

One of the questions the sages ask Bharata is what is a performance or production (*prayoga*) like? In the earlier chapters Bharata has just referred to two or three performances of his before the Gods Brahmā and Śiva and then explained at length what was meant by acting. In between, he has described the theatre-house and also the stage. In connection with the latter he had said that the stage had to be different in dimensions according to the different types of plays. And later the individual acting was discussed. But the performance as a whole (or what we call the production) in which stage, acting, stage-movements story and audience lead to one total effect has not been referred to till now and the sages wanted to know that too. So in chapter XIII the *Nāṭyaśāstra* describes the stagecraft, i.e., the element other than the author's story, and actor's acting that gives an artistic individuality and leads to one total effect of the performance. This element consists in the art of relating all the constituent elements in a particular manner. Or rather, it consists in choosing the various constituents in such manner and such proportion that an intended artistic effect is produced on the audience.

Now, to begin with, Bharata (or the producer) selects the play. The first performance was before gods and demons.

Was it an accident? Was it deliberate? Did Bharata intend to win God Brahmā's favour? Apparently, it was none of these things. Bharata selected a story which was well-known to his audience or it was one in which, the audience, themselves being actors, were expected to feel interested. Even the disturbance created by demons was a compliment to Bharata. It meant that his play was not only understood but felt, re-experienced by his audience. That is why he did not drop the idea of producing dramas but rather devised a way in which dramas could be performed undisturbed.

After selecting a play, the next thing is to decide how to produce it—i.e., whether to produce it as it is or on a stage. To put it in the words of Bharata, one must know if the play could be taken to an audience as a *lokadharmī* or a *nāṭyadharmī*.

"If it is to be read as it was written, with no modifications of any kind, without bodily movements and just like any piece of news or information, with many men and women looking and behaving in the usual everyday manner, then it is a *lokadharmī*; if, however, with long sentences, facial expressions, bodily movements and voice intonations, with heavenly as well as human beings then it is a *nāṭyadharmī*" (XIII, 66-69).

Similarly, the play has to be considered from another point of view. Is it going to be one where the story and the characters are men and women we find in ordinary life? Or god and demons with their super-human personalities and actions? Would the play show everyday life of pain and pleasure? Or of wickedness, cruelty, deceit, etc.? According to the answers to these questions, particular requirements would be inevitable starting from the size of the stage to the time of performance and to the number and nature of audience to be expected. Broadly, *Nāṭyaśāstra* recognises, from this point of view, two kinds of productions, (1) *sukumāra* and the other

(2) *āviddha.* It is difficult to translate, these words to give the correct sense intended by the *Nāṭyaśāstra.* But it is interesting to note that of the ten forms of plays recognised by Bharata (and to be discussed by us later) four, viz., *samavakāra, ḍīma, vyāyoga* and *īhāmṛga* are to be produced in the *āviddha* style and *nāṭaka, prakaraṇa, bhāṇa, vīthi, aṅka* and *nāṭikā* (this last is not one of the ten forms) in the *sukumāra* style. In the *āviddha* style the methods (*vṛtti*) would be *sāttvatī* and *ārabhaṭī,* i.e., plenty of movements and actions and fights and magic, etc., while in the *sukumāra* style the *vṛttis* would be *bhāratī* and *kaiśikī,* dialogues, emotional acting, dancing and singing, etc.

As a matter of fact, says the author, according to producers there is a fourfold distinction (broadly speaking) in the ways of people. This way which he calls *pravṛtti* is distinguished by the dress, language, costume, etc., of people of different countries (XIII, 32 and following prose lines). The world, to the author of the *Nāṭyaśāstra,* was India itself in which he recognises the fourfold division as southern (*dākṣiṇātya*), western (*āvantī*), northern (*pāñcālī*) and eastern (*coudramāgadhī*); this, he says, is a very broad distinction. Not only different *vṛttis* and styles are associated with each region but even some of the stage conventions are different. (XIII, 33ff., 45-48); production must follow the style and the *vṛtti* current in the customs of the people of the region in which the play is produced.

But there are other things to be considered as the play is put on the stage. It has been repeatedly said in the book that a drama is a mirror to men and society. Does that mean that all the actions of men and women are just imitated or reproduced on the stage? The stage, as such, is a strictly limited area in which everything is shown. In Indian dramas, there are not the three unities as are found in the Western drama.

How are different countries, even different locales and different times shown on the Indian stage?

To begin with Bharata has either established or recognised certain conventions applicable to the stage of all regions of the country. It is true that these conventions are not always accepted or followed except by second-rate dramatists but they are helpful in producing plays of writers who do not refer to them; or perhaps, the Indian dramatists write their plays according to the rules of rhetorics (canons of literature) and *sūtradhāra* or producer was responsible for putting them on the stage according to the rules of the stage.

In the beginning verses of chapter XIII the author tells us how the stage-area is to be divided into different ones to convey the sense of different scenes of locales. He says, (XIII, 1-4):

> I have already mentioned three types of play-houses and stage; bearing in mind their mutual difference, one should employ on *kakṣā* arrangement;
> I also have mentioned two doors from *nepathya-gṛha* to the stage; in the centre of these two doors, musical instruments should be placed.

The word *kakṣā* has not be translated above; it is not so easy. Literally it would mean 'a small enclosure, a small room', etc. But here the meaning seems to be a specialised one. It has been shown that the stage is divided into three compartments, the *nepathya-gṛha,* the *raṅga-śīrṣa* and the *raṅga-pīṭha.* This last one is nearest to the audience in a *vikṛṣṭa* or an oblong play-house which is the normal one preferred by Bharata; the *raṅga-śīrṣa* is behind it and on a slight height; and the *nepathya-gṛha* is the last and farthest from the audience. This *nepathya-gṛha* has two doors at either ends. One is used only for characters coming right up to the front on the *raṅga-*

pīṭha, and the other exclusively as an entry to the *raṅga-śīrṣa.* Actually these two, viz., the *śīrṣa* and the *pītha* represent what we now call (two) levels. Characters considered *nīca* (i.e., low in status) make their entry on the *pīṭha* while the high ones (like the hero and the heroine) on the *śīrṣa.* But even on each level itself, distinction is preserved, e.g., on the *raṅga-pīṭha,* as required by the particular scene, one side (or end) may represent the back door of the palace and the other one the palace garden. But this difference is not conveyed by any special device like a curtain or any other object; it is the actor who by his movements tells us that just coming out of the palace back door he (or she) is going to the palace garden. Thus the distinction is established by further going in a circular movement (*parikramaṇa*) and moving to the new spot.

> The distinction between the different *kakṣās* shall be conveyed by a circular movement on the *raṅga-pīṭha*; by the *parikramaṇa* another *kakṣā* may be said to have been established (XIII, 3).

Those characters who make their entry earlier are supposed to be inside, and those coming later outside the *kakṣā* (XIII, 9). As the character enters on the proper 'level' and before it meets another character, the lone entrant must face southwards, backstage being considered east. The exit must be by the same 'door' by which the entry has been made.

Now, the *parikramaṇa* is also used to denote nearness or distance between two spot (e.g., with 2 or 3 very quick *parikramaṇas* the character can say that it has come the whole distance from one town to another) (XIII, 17). Not only that, by appropriate gaits and gestures even travel by chariots or aeroplanes may be conveyed to the audience.

With this arrangement on the stage there was no need to place any stage property which also is a device to inform the locale to the audience. On the other hand, the author is against this practice (XXI, 190), though he refers in the passage to only heavy things. It is interesting to observe the devices which Bharata suggests to convey a locale without the trouble of putting up any sets as we know them now. In the absence of unities like those of time and place, in one and the same play the story may continue over different seasons and the incidents happen in different places. In the Sanskrit plays we invariably find this feature. What Bharata says (XXV, 76-77), for example, regarding the stage arrangement in such cases is interesting:

> Tall mountains and trees may be suggested by outstretched hands and hands lifted over the head;
> A sea or an expansive lake, etc., may be shown by hands thrown out in the *patākā* gesture.

The absence of any sets or property (except the implements or accessories associated with certain characters) is either the result or the cause of the absence of a certain or any other external device to convey change of scenes or acts. The performance was probably continuous and uninterrupted from the beginning to the end. The change of place, time, etc., was conveyed by the conventions like *parikramaṇa, kakṣā* arrangements and by the characters themselves. The progress of the story too was conveyed by devices which could be considered more as literary than as stage conventions. We shall discuss them later in connection with play-writing. Here it is interesting to observe the ease and the cleverness of Bharata in utilising gestures, poses, movements as important stage-techniques. Even the various seasons can be shown on the stage but in a symbolical way, to such an extent that surroundings are conveyed as suiting the mood of the characters (and not necessarily) the actual time of the year the incident concerned would have happened (XXV, 37-39).

In the technical terms of his own *rasa* theory, Bharata says, "*vibhāva* (stimulus), *anubhāva* (bodily reaction) and *bhāva* (the emotional reaction) are to be acted by men and women" (XXV, 45).

If the actor is as talented as Bharata required him to be, it is not at all necessary to crowd the stage, to the further detraction of the audience, with a number of articles and objects.

Finally, one more duty of the producer (or the director) may be mentioned, Bharata opens chapter XXXV with the following words:

> Now I shall describe the allotment of the different parts and what is one's duty in this regard and how it should be executed.

Since Bharata has, by this time, standardized the characters into definite types, in this chapter, he prescribes the qualifications of actors to play particular parts. As a rule, in fairness to the requirements of a dramatic performance, casting should be done according to the age, appearance, etc. (XXV, 3-15) so that the director will have no troubles later on. If, however, one fulfilling the requirements is not available, then (only) the director, in his discretion, might choose one who could not express emotions with proper gestures (XXXV, 19). Further, in the same chapter, Bharata also describes make-up man, costumes man, property man and so on including the *sūtradhāra* and the *kuśīlava* (an instrumentalist) and tells us the exact duties of each one of these.

This, in short, is what Bharata understands and describes in connection with what we now know as stagecraft. If we look critically at the various things that Bharata has to say we are compelled to feel how far the art of drama production had advanced and had been organized. It is apparent that the popular stage, when the *Nāṭyaśāstra* was composed, was not so much a place of artistic medium of education as of sheer entertainment. Nor was there any uniformity in either the stage-representations or the styles of acting. Bharata himself is compelled to confess that a fourfold distinction, on a broad basis, had to be admitted; probably, in details, there were more divergences. Secondly, in most of these plays of the popular stage, the majority dealt with low (*hīna*) or *prākṛt* characters; the usual style of the story was also either low humour or low erotic sentiment or sometime *adbhuta*, i.e., fantastic magic, black art, etc. Another interesting feature of these *uparūpakas* as they were later called is plenty of dancing and music. The plays were too short, many no more than one-acts. These plays were performed on festival days and looking to the type of persons that the actors and the audience constituted we are not surprised that Bharata mentions of disturbances—though symbolically only during his first production. The story in *Nāṭyaśāstra* puts the very first production on the day of Indra's festival. Indra is the god of rain.

Apparently, play-performance served two purposes, if we could judge from what used to happen in the villages till recently; on the one hand, it was a great enjoyment after the harvest days and, on the other, it was kind of worship of Indra for blessing rains during the following season. These plays were mostly produced in the open as far as the audience was concerned; for the actors there was a raised platform and a *nepathya-gṛha* below it with theoretically two entries—one from behind the platform and the other from the front through the audience—mostly in plays where gods and demons took part; otherwise, two kinds of entries were technically distinguished, in one case characters (particularly 'low' or subordinate ones) entering from the *nepathya-gṛha* from behind the platform and taking their place in the stage-front while the other entry reserved for 'high' characters was in the same way but concealed behind a piece of cloth till they took their place in the *raṅga-śirṣa* part of the stage. Before the *Nāṭyaśāstra,* apparently, there were no theatre-houses as such nor a specially built stage; plays were performed either in the temple-yard or on any raised place with open space all round. The *Nāṭyaśāstra* seems to have taken the initiative in thinking of a specially constructed theatre and stage and further proposed that according to the difference in the story and characters the size and shape of the stage should vary. But the greatest revolution which was effected by the *Nāṭyaśāstra* was to give artistic form and content to what was still then a vulgar medium or source of entertainment; it was this which later helped the development of drama by making it possible for kings and rich persons to patronise it. Whether Bharata wrote himself the entire *Nāṭyaśāstra* or whether Bharata was just the leader of a movement to reform the stage, and *Nāṭyaśāstra* represents his views as recollected later by a number of his followers or whether Bharata was, as the word came to mean later on, an actor and a producer with new ideas and later on some scholars edited these ideas in his name—it is futile for us to discuss. But one thing is certain. Within the text of *Nāṭyaśāstra* which, as it is now, is just like an attic where all things are dumped in a heap, it is possible to find something historical about the origin and growth of Indian drama. What we must marvel at is the brilliant intuition or intellect of the author or authors which has given us ideas that hold true even today. But Bharata's greatest achievement was in pointing out that the play is the most important thing since not mere entertainment but enlightenment was (or should be) the final objective of a drama. A drama was considered *kāvya* or literature and then distinguished as *dṛśya kāvya,* i.e., literature that could also be seen and understood and there is no doubt that Bharata or the views attributed to him were mainly instrumental in putting drama on that high pedestal. Bharata was not satisfied with insisting that drama was literature; he analysed it to show how and why it was literature and further he gave rules to guide authors as to how audio-visual literature should be written. Before we discuss these things we shall see the structural uniformity that Bharata gave to a stage-representation (*rūpaka*). This is discussed by him under the heading of Ten *Rūpakas* or ten varieties of stage-representations.

8

Ten Forms of Stage-Representations

Indian dramaturgy does not recognise any classification based on the end of the drama or on the fact whether, finally the characters live happily or succumb to a vain struggle against almost impossible odds. For reasons to be explained later there is no such thing as a happy or a sad ending. As a matter of fact, there is no ending at all as such since life in our outlook is an indestructible phenomenon and life and death one unending stream of continuity. Besides, the Indian tradition believes in a superhuman power called fate and all the joys and sorrows of life are inevitable or predestined due to the laws of fate. A drama, therefore, in Indian tradition does not mean or convey any conflict. Of course, good and evil do exist side by side and god is there to destroy the evil and human beings are either the battle-ground or the spectators of this fight. For this reason, in Indian drama evil things like death, etc., are not shown on the stage; from one point of view there is no such thing as death and, from another, anything created must die. What then is the object of drama apart from pure entertainment which Bharata does not accept? Drama, says Bharata, is literature and like other forms of literature such as poetry, etc., its object is to show men the proper way to live, a way in which you live and behave so that in your next life you are born a still better man. Whatever drama Bharata found existing before him was not literature in this sense, was not open to the high and the low (since the former found it not in good taste and Bharata insisted that drama must be open to all) and even to those with whom it was popular it did not help by giving proper guidance (and Bharata insisted that drama should be the fifth Veda as far as knowledge giving was considered). So, before formulating his own *śāstra,* Bharata studied the different forms that existed and, like a practical man, instead of shouting against them he recognised them with limitations and evolved new forms based on them. But actually he tricked his public by saying that the new forms he evolved were not new but actually the origin and source of the other forms current. The ten forms (*daśa rūpaka*) if understood in this light, would give us a historical perspective.

In chapter XVIII, these ten forms are described.

"I shall tell you about the ten *rūpakas,* their names, their content (*krama*) and their performance" (XVIII, 1) says Bharata, and then straightaway mentions their names in the following order: (1) *nāṭaka,* (2) *prakaraṇa,* (3) *aṅka,* (4) *vyāyoga,* (5) *bhāṇa,* (6) *samavakāra,* (7) *vīthi,* (8) *prahasana,* (9) *ḍīma,* and (10) *īhāmṛga.* The order in which they are mentioned need not be given more importance since metrical reasons are usually more responsible for such things, unless the author mentions anything to the contrary. There is no such mention here. On the other hand, we shall find that, accident or otherwise, the order is interesting because the newly evolved forms are put first and earlier ones last.

After mentioning the names Bharata gives the reason for this kind of a distinction. What is the basis on which different forms are recognised? The bases or the mother-sources as Bharata puts it (XVIII, 4) are what are called *vṛttis.* This word *vṛtti* is one of the many misused Sanskrit words. Even in its own form it is used to convey a variety of meaning and with prepositions like *pra* or *ā* or *ni*, etc., it flourishes in chaotic vagueness. In the *Nāṭyaśāstra* and books based or commenting on it, *vṛtti* is recognised in a technical sense. Broadly speaking it conveys the sense of 'a style of production.' But in the present context it does not seem to be used in that sense. *Vṛttis* here are mentioned as the source of different types of plays.

In chapter XX there is a fanciful legend to explain the origin of *vṛttis* themselves. It is said that once the two demons, Madhu and Kaiṭabha, picked up a fight with God Viṣṇu (or Kṛṣṇa). They started not only pounding him with their knees and fists but also shouting insulting words. Seeing that God Brahmā said to God Viṣṇu, "what is this *bhāratī* behaviour (*vṛtti*) with words, each leading to the other?" This is one of the poorest explanations as can be understood by XX, 11, wherein the word *bhāratī* is being related to *atibhāra,* which means, extremely heavy; similarly, in the following verses more (*vṛttis*) are explained, (1) *sāttvatī,* fantastically derived from the word, *sattva*; (2) *kaiśikī,* equally fanciful by explaining in relation to the word *keśa* meaning hair (the fighting god is described in XX, 13 as tying his hair); and (3) finally, the *ārabhaṭī.* And then each is given a restricted meaning, e.g., *bhāratī,* expressing through words; *sāttvatī,* expressing through words and gestures; *kaiśikī,* expressing in graceful movements; and *ārabhaṭī,* expressing in violent movements. The author of this fancy further let himself be tempted by the idea that there were four Vedas, and there were four *vṛttis.* So why not relate each *vṛtti* to a corresponding Veda. In XX, 24, he tells us that *bhāratī* was derived from *Ṛgveda, sāttvatī* from *Yajurveda, kaiśikī* from *Sāmaveda,* and *ārabhaṭī* from *Atharvaveda.* This reminds of I, 17, in which, speaking of the origin of drama as the fifth Veda created out of the four Vedas, the author tells us that words (prose and poetry) were taken from *Ṛgveda*, music from *Sāmaveda*, acting from *Yajurveda* and *rasa* from *Atharvaveda*. If we put the two passages together (one is almost tempted to give the analogy of *A=B, A=C, ∴ B=C*), we can say that *bhāratī vṛtti*=prose and poetry; *sāttvatī vṛtti*=singing (and dancing) and *ārabhaṭī vṛtti*=final enjoyment or entertaining activities. Looking closely at the above, we almost feel cheated, because in spite of all that fanciful and legendary narration, we are only told that drama was born out of imitation, singing, dancing and words!

But the cheating does not end there. The author takes as seriously through the definition of each of these four, the divisions and sub-divisions of each (XX, 25-63) and then innocently concludes the chapter by saying (XX, 66). "I have explained the *abhinaya*, that is the end of (i.e., based on) a *vṛtti* and now I shall explain *āhārya abhinaya* based on *nepathya*."

As a matter of fact the whole chapter is out of context since the *vṛttis*, if they were the source of ten forms of drama, should have been described in chapter XVIII where the latter are described.

It is obvious that whoever introduced the explanation of these *vṛttis* was himself not clear about the underlying idea. Let us say that the original Bharata did not go beyond suggesting that drama was born out of natural tendencies of man to imitate, to sing and to dance and to mimick the talk and actions of others, and further these tendencies were employed both for one's own and also other people's amusement. This would have been an honest but not an impressive, much less a dignified effort to understand the origin of drama, particularly because God Brahmā was already involved in it. So something divine or superhuman or mystical had to be invented and the story of the demons Madhu and Kaiṭabha was invented. But as we has seen it was too thin to conceal an honest guess behind it. The verses XX, 25-63 that describe the divisions and sub-divisions of our *vṛttis* seem to be a still later effort of giving the legend a semblance of credulity. For example, *bhāratī vṛtti* has four divisions, viz., *prarocanā, āmukham, vīthi* and *prahasanam.* The first one is the praise of gods or flattery of the audience by the *sūtradhāra* as part of *pūrvaraṅga, āmukham* is part of the prologue where the *sūtradhāra* by himself or in dialogue with his assistants or *vidūṣaka* introduces the story (the introduction, further, can be done in five different ways); *vīthi* is beginning the story with a character or an incident off-stage and *prahasanam* would be doing the same thing in a humorous way. All this elaborate cleverness, as we see, does not add either to the importance or to the explanation of the *bhāratī vṛtti.* A similar kind of scholasticism may be expected on the other three *vṛttis.*

The difference in the four *vṛttis* is reflected in the difference in the type of plays. In Sanskrit literary tradition, a drama is supposed to take a definite shape according to the plot and the hero and the *rasa.* As seen above, distinction like tragedy or comedy or romance does not obtain in Sanskrit plays. Every play must have a *rasa* and everyone of the eight *rasas* bring enjoyment to the audience. Now a *rasa* depends on the type of the story and the sort of hero. Therefore, hero (*netā*), story (*vastu*) and *rasa* (artistic enjoyment) constitute the three essential ingredients of a drama. According to the difference in these respects the ten forms are to be recognised. For this reason it is worthwhile to study the ten forms with reference to the three constituent elements.

1. *Nāṭaka* (XVIII, 10ff): The story is well-known; royal sage or *dhīroddhāta* is the hero; and the *rasa* is either

śṛṅgāra (love) or *vīra* (heroic). Five to seven acts in length.

2. *Prakaraṇam* (XVIII, 96ff): The story is made up by the writer; the hero is a brāhmaṇa or a minister or a merchant; main *rasa* is *śṛṅgāra* (love). Five to ten acts in length.
3. *Aṅka* (XVIII, 146ff): Well-known or not well-known story; ordinary man is the hero; *rasa* is pathos. One act.
4. *Vyāyoga* (XVIII, 142): Well-known story; not a divine being but a royal sage is the hero; *rasa* any except humour and love. One act.
5. *Bhāṇa* (XVIII, 160ff): Story built by the author; a rogue (only one character in this play) is the hero; *rasa* is *śṛṅgāra* (love) or *vīra* (heroic). One act.
6. *Samavakāra* (XVIII, 130ff): Well-known story: gods and demons are heroes; heroism is the principal *rasa*. Three act.
7. *Vīthi* (XVIII, 164ff): Story built by the dramatist; one or two characters; and main *rasa* is love. One act.
8. *Prahasana* (XVIII, 154ff): Imaginary story.
9. *Ḍīma* (XVIII, 136ff): Well-known story; gods and demons; *rasa* is probably *adbhuta* or *bībhatsa* or *vīra* because of magic, witchcraft, fighting, etc. Four acts.
10. *Īhāmṛga* (XVIII, 130ff): Mixed story of gods and men. Man is hero; *rasa* the same as in *vyāyoga*. Four acts.

Now for a moment, let us go back to the story of Bharata's first production of play, since that, according to Bharata, is the beginning or origin of drama. The very first play which Bharata produced is classified by him as a *samavakāra* (IV, 30). A *samavakāra* as we have seen above, has a well-known story. Bharata's play was about the well-known story of the churning of the ocean by gods and demons and their find of *amṛta* (nectar); the story describes a battle, so the sentiment is *vīra* or heroic. If, however, we look closely at the details of this type of drama, we find some other interesting features.

To begin with, this is a story in which there is no individual hero; all the gods are on one side and all the demons on the other; as we know the story, we also know that throughout the play there would be crowd scenes, shouting, battles, deceit, etc. As a matter of fact, there would be less difference between the form of a story and the form of a drama—with all these actions. It is, therefore, very likely that the early 'plays' were more action and loud behaviour as in a *samavakāra* than any artistic representations of feelings and character. After the performance of this *samavakāra,* Bharata was asked to give a special show for God Śiva and his henchmen. Bharata says that he produced a play called *Tripura-dāha* which, according to him, belonged to the *ḍīma* type (IV, 10). Strangely enough *ḍīma* is not much different from a *samavakāra.* Here too the story is a well-known one; there is no individual here but, as in a *samavakāra,* there are gods and demons and battles and in addition devils, magic and witchcraft as well. If *samavakāra* is in three, *ḍīma* is in four acts. But apart from that the distinction is just one of degrees; *ḍīma* probably is louder than *samavakāra* and there could be no suggestion of any effort at drama as an art. These two types, the earliest according to Bharata, are nothing more than an imitation of actions of a well-known story, and because of the predominance of crowds less of what could be called of dramatic dialogue. In neither of these is there any music or dance and it is very obvious that these were entertainments of the rough people, by the rough people and for the rough people. Of the ten recognised forms there is one more which like *ḍīma* and *samavakāra* is less of a drama and more of a story that is enacted by imitating speech and actions. It is *īhāmṛga* where instead of the demons there are human beings (men) pitted against the gods. Man as against a god is the hero, and god is a foil (*prati-nāyaka*); the quarrel between men and the gods is for a women of the gods; the behaviour of the latter lacks dignity and propriety; and naturally the sentiment is *śṛṅgāra*. Except this last, *īhāmṛga* is similar to *vyāyoga*. But again there are crowds in this place, there is plenty of anger, disturbances, quarrels, etc., but no battles and no deaths. If in *samavakāra* and *ḍīma* the stories were already known, in *īhāmṛga* it is built by the writer's imagination.

The foregoing three forms seem, therefore, to be the earliest forms of dramatic entertainment and, as could be seen, they are very crude both in story-building and stage-representation. Bharata seems to have been correct in putting *samavakāra* and *ḍīma* as the two earliest forms. Though he does not refer to any other form in a way that could be construed historically, the definition and description of *īhāmṛga* leads us to the conclusion that this also must have been one of the earliest forms.

Drama in which characters with individuality live and move can be detected to some small extent in three other forms, viz., *bhāṇa, prahasana* and *vīthi*. These three are all short, one-acts to be exact. There is not much of a story as such, well-known or imagined by the writer, though the last one makes a claim to contain a story built up by the writer. More important, however, is the fact that all the three show an advance on the first three already discussed. This advance is in two respects: one, as against crowds in the first group these three deal with one or two (maximum) characters and these are neither gods nor demons nor royal sages but low-born rogues from the living world; two, the sentiment also is low *śṛṅgāra,* low humour or melodramatic heroics. Drama may be said to lie hidden like a sown seen in these three. The purpose of these forms is purely to entertain the audience. But that entertainment is not merely by narrating or representing facts known from a story but by putting facts in relation to each other in a way deliberately giving pleasure. Because of *śṛṅgāra* (the sentiment of love) music and dance also, of a type to suit the general quality, would add to the entertainment. But even at this level, drama is not only mere entertainment but one of low taste.

When we come to two other one-acts, viz., *aṅka* and *vyāyoga* we find a difference of significance for the first time. In the first one which is called *utsṛṣṭikāṅka* (since the word *aṅka* is more used in the sense of 'an act') there is one hero and he is a man and an ordinary man at that. The story is the writer's own or a well-known one. Now if the story of an ordinary man is to be a well-known one, it must be one in tradition or history or legend. But apart from that, the character study of an ordinary man is for the first time, presented on the stage. That there could be no low *śṛṅgāra* or low humour is shown by the fact that the sentiment is pathos—showing particularly a number of female characters wailing; *vyāyoga* on the other hand, has more male than female characters. Here too the story is a well-known one and a royal sage or a divine being (in contrast to *aṅka*) is the hero. And also unlike as in the *aṅka*—there shall be a battle but it is for reasons other than a woman.

In all these eight forms, one finds not only lack of development but some kind of crudity. Those which are attempts at introducing an artistic tendency are too short to be called drama and/or too narrative to be a *dṛśya kāvya* or even too unimaginative to be any sort of *kāvya*. Those which are longer like *samavakāra* are nothing more than shows for grown up children; these foregoing eight represent an earlier type of stage-entertainment and the only progress in them was from fanciful crudity to a consciousness of crudity. As a rule there was no imaginative composition of a play as such except the story of gods and demons and devils; even when one character was the centre (i.e., hero) of the story, that character would be a 'royal sage' suggesting that fantasy would have more scope than art or actual life. Apart from low characters there was very little that was taken from actual life. In short, all the eight forms were nothing more than an attempt at mere entertainment by mimicking stories full of actions from mythology.

The remaining two, viz., *nāṭaka* and *prakaraṇa* are so violently different from all the others that one feels justified in holding that these two must have been the deliberate creation of Bharata. There is hardly anything that could be traced back to the earlier forms except the fact that the stories of these two are also of the same type, viz., either well-known (i.e., from mythology and Purāṇas) or made up by the writer's imagination but from out of tradition like legends or history. Retaining a story that would be known to the audience, Bharata introduced entirely new features without making his audience suspect any break from tradition.

It is not so much the story or the hero or the heroine, but the construction of the story that, according to Bharata and rightly so, should be considered important. In the earlier plays there was little by way of arranging the episodes in a manner in which not only continuity but a kind to tempo was built. For this reason there were more incidents or episodes than a story connected out of them. Secondly, Bharata provided an objective to the play. It is not merely to see and feel entertained by the actions of gods and demons and even human beings. The purpose of a drama should be to show us how the greater or the wiser people behaved under given circumstances. This indirectly gave us knowledge, showed us the way to behave properly or correctly in life. That is the main reason why Bharata prescribes that a hero in a *nāṭaka* should be a dignified, noble, large-hearted man with a refined taste and the one in a *prakaraṇa* a brāhmaṇa or a merchant or a minister. He goes further than that. In all the earlier forms there is no such person as a heroine. But in these two not only a heroine is there but she is as cultured as the hero himself. With such heroes and heroines, low humour and vulgar love-scenes were automatically ruled out and Bharata could say with pride that now, "parents could see a dramatic performance in company of their son and daughter-in-law" (XXII, 288).

As we have seen earlier, Bharata has made deliberate efforts to see that a drama and a dramatic performance must first be a work of art and then literature, our guide and friend and philosopher. We shall now see how the new drama was to be written and constructed to achieve this object.

9

Play-Construction

Writers, a common sense all over the world would have it, are not only born but are also made. Sanskrit books on rhetorics (literature and appreciation) recognise study of classics along with experience as one of the causes for literary composition. Bharata, always practical minded as we have seen, has not only accepted this but provided for it. Just as he had formulated rules for the guidance of actors and producers, so he has described in detail how a good play could (and should) be written. To begin with we must accept his thesis that drama should aim at instruction through entertainment. By entertainment, as we shall see later, he means not what is commonly understood but an artistic sense of enjoyment ending as complete relaxation. Secondly, a story or a chief character in terms of a number of incidents or episodes or actions is to be the skeleton round which the body of the play is to be built or, in his own words, the prerequisites of a play to be written are *vastu* (plot), *netā* (hero) and *rasa* (sentiment).

One of the later writers in the tradition of Bharata has said about a play performance that its duration must be not more that a *yāma* (three hours), then only it is seen with unabated interest (*rāga-vardhana*). Śubhaṅkara, a writer possibly of sixteenth century and author of a book called *Saṅgīta-dāmodara*, further adds, "a longer play would produce indifference (*virāgajanakam*)—therefore, it should be avoided." The reason for quoting this is to show that drama which must be a representation of actual life (*lokānucarita*) has to be, if Bharata's definition is fulfilled, a selection of incidents since within a limited time it would not be possible to show life in all its details. The *Abhijñāna Śākuntalam* by Kālidāsa, for example, takes up the love-story of Duṣyanta and Śakuntalā over a number of years and from beginning to end. But this is done in only seven acts, each act dealing with a selected episode, and each episode succeeding the other and taking the story further. So it is not merely a story that would serve as plot but one which is built by a series of main or significant episodes. Of these series of incidents the writer should fix up which shall be the first and which the last. Usually there is not much difficulty about the last since the author should know what he wants to say or show finally. This final episode or end is more important since the beginning one would depend on it. "This is what or how it happened" is the last thing or the *iti-vṛtta* (a sort of Q.E.D.). This *iti-vṛtta* is the body or the main substance of a drama, says Bharata (XIX, 1). Now one must select episodes that lead to Q.E.D. and, oftentimes, that also help establish the Q.E.D. The *vastu* or the plot is the story-part contained in from the first to the last episode. The construction of the play (i.e., development of the plot) from the first episode to the last is a well-thought out procedure, no different from a logical syllogism.

To begin with there would be the main plot in which the episodes are concerned with the main character or the hero. Since the ending is directly concerned with the hero only he is called *adhikārin* i.e., one who is entitled to the final result and the main plot which directly concerns him is *ādhikārikām*.

But as in usual life so in drama no man is alone in the sense of not coming into contact with others. Naturally, the hero also would be having friends or associations whose actions would affect his. To the extent that the hero's achievement is helped by these others, their story is called *prāsaṅgika*, incidental and when it runs so parallel as to merge its end with that of the hero, it is called *patākā*—major sub-plot; but when that story is just an isolated episode it is called *prakarī*, i.e., minor sub-plot. In other words, the main plot is made not only interesting but one that would arouse our curiosity and appreciation by inter-weaving it with a 'sub-episode'. The main with the subsidiary plot constitutes the raw material out of which the development of the story is to be constructed. At the end of the story the hero is supposed to realise (this is the *iti-vṛtta*), either one, two or more from among *dharma* (merit), *artha* (wealth) and *kāma* (desired end).

Once we have the beginning and the end, the writer's art consists in the logical artistry in which the hero leads himself to the final achievement. This process is analysed by Bharata along two lines; one, from the point of the hero himself, all the actions that he deliberately does to achieve the end; and, secondly, from the point of view of circumstances independent of the hero which contribute to the achievement. But in general terms, this analysis sounds almost like a passage in a book on philosophy. But actually, it is simple to work and understand through a given example. Let us take the example of Kālidāsa's *Abhijñāna Śākuntalam*. The final achievement in this story is the union in love of Duṣyanta (the hero) and Śakuntalā (the heroine). In the first Duṣyanta finds that, unknown to himself, he has trespassed into the hermitage of the sage Kaṇva. This is an independent, outside circumstance since there was no deliberate intention on his part. But after learning of the circumstance he makes up his mind to go and pay his respects to the sage. Now both these incidents combine together to give an opening to the story. In the technology of the *Nāṭyaśāstra* straying into Kaṇva's hermitage is the *bīja* (seed) and Duṣyanta's wilful action to go to the sage to pay his respects is the *ārambha* (beginning) and the two circumstances combining to start the love-story is the *sandhi* (joining, combining) called *mukha* (lit. = face, opening first, etc.). In this manner the different (five in all) stages of the development of the story are described as five *sandhis* and each *sandhi* means the joining of an outward circumstance with a voluntary action of the hero. The outward circumstance is known as *artha-prakṛti* and hero's voluntary actions are known as *avasthā* and five of the former joining with the corresponding five of the latter give us five *sandhis*. The five *avasthās* are as follows:

(1) *ārambha* (beginning); (2) *prayatma* (making effort); (3) *prāptyāśā* (meeting of obstacles); (4) *niyatāpti* (removal of obstacles); (5) *phalāgama* (denouement). The five *artha-prakṛti* are: (1) *bīja* (seed); (2) *bindu* (contributory incident); (3) *patākā* (major sub-plot); (4) *prakarī* (minor sub-plot or stray incident); and (5) *kārya* (denouement). Lastly, the five *sandhis* are these: (1) *mukha* (opening one joining *ārambha* and *bīja*); (2) *pratimukha* raising hopes and combining *yatna* and *bindu*; (3) *garbha* raising doubt in which *prāptyāśā* and *patākā* combine; (4) *sāvamarśa* situation under control; here are joined *nīyataptī* and *prakarī*; and finally (5) *nīrvahana* conclusion—*phalāgama* and *kārya* combine.

Let us, for a moment, forget the meticulous tone of scholasticism shown by Bharata in evolving a hair-splitting technology to explain how a story is (to be) dramatised. Let us go behind the curtain, so to say, and find out what is the basic principle of the show. To begin with and as could be verified from almost all the Sanskrit plays, no play has a story unknown to the audience. Even when Bharata says that in a particular form of drama the story is *kavi-kalpita,* i.e., imagined by the poet, he seems to convey the idea not that the story itself is the invention of the writer but the writer has used his imagination in dramatising it. This was not done in the earliest plays. By providing for two kinds of sub-plots Bharata gives a dramatist scope to use his imagination.

The more important thing to be noticed is that the prescription of Bharata for drama-building is mainly based on the traditional Hindu outlook on life. Man is not a free agent and he is governed by the laws of *karma;* if at all he is free, it is in a restricted sense because if his past determines his present, his present, if properly managed, could shape his future. Due to this law of *karma,* joys and sorrows are to be equally taken in his stride. The main reason is that man is not the sole architect of his fortune. There are more things outside his ken and control that happen and happen to shape his destiny. It is this outlook on life that is responsible for not giving us, in Indian drama, any tragedy in the Western sense. When fortune favours you, all things happen for your good; when fortune does not favour you, it serves no purpose to fight against it. So, outside happenings play as much a part in our life as things we ourselves do apparently with a deliberate purpose. *Avasthā,* one's own deliberate actions and *artha-prakṛti,* outside happenings must go together if the final result is to be achieved. A lover may do everything heroic and adventurous but unless he is destined to win his beloved he will not succeed. And in case he does not win here he does not commit suicide; at the worst, he will be raving and at the best he will try to induce Dame Fortune to smile on him. The obstacles that beset his path in the third *artha-prakṛti* are due to the third *avasthā,* viz., *patākā,* in other words, the obstacles come from an outside source. Then in the next *avasthā,* another outside agency, viz., the *artha-prakṛti* called *prakarī* helps the removal of obstacles.

Because of this thought-process being at the background, the characters in a play, according to Bharata, cannot have much of an individuality. It is not necessary either since ultimately they are the pawns of Fate. It is not surprising, therefore, to find not only heroes and heroines but even the minor characters defined in great details. The hero (*nāyaka*), for example, is first defined in general way as one who is "polite, loving, generous, diligent, good in talk, popular, pure-minded, firm-minded, good conversationalist, young, intelligent, enthusiastic, self-respecting, handsome, learned, brave, religious-minded and scion of a good family." But that is only the total picture. Looked at closely, we find heroes of four kinds: (1) *dhīra-lalita*, 'one who does not worry, is interested in arts, happy and soft-hearted'; (2) *dhīra-śānta*, one who has all the general qualities and 'is always calm-minded and a twice-born'; (3) *dhīrodātta*, 'one who has high character, great dignity, forgiving nature, does not brag, does not waver, is master of vanity and of a persisting nature'; and (4) *dhīroddhata*, 'one bursting with arrogance and envy, scheming, vain, fickle-minded, obstinate and bragging'. Even this elaborateness does not seem to satisfy Bharata. Most of the stories of Sanskrit plays are love-stories, so the hero of a love-story is further distinguished by four different characteristics (*lakṣaṇas*); (1) he is *anukūla-lakṣaṇa* (conveniently placed) if he has only one heroine; (2) having more than one heroine if he is sympathetic to the elderly one he is called *dakṣiṇa-lakṣaṇa* (polite or courteous); (3) he is called cunning (*śat-lakṣaṇa*) if he secretly works against the interests of the elderly heroine; and finally (4) he is called brazen-faced (*dhṛṣṭa-lakṣaṇa*) if he does not conceal and openly vaunts before the elderly one his dalliance with the younger one. But luckily, now and then even as a relief from the boredom of his love-affairs, the hero may find himself faced with some other routine problems. On such occasions he may have to show qualities other than those enumerated above and according to these qualities (as *śobhā, vilāsa, mādhurya, gāmbhīrya, sthairya, tejas, lalita,* and *audārya*) he is further classified into eight types. It must be expected in this context that heroines too would be classified first on their own 'merits' and next *vis-à-vis* the hero's attitude towards them. In the first category there are three types: (1) *svā* or *svīyā*, i.e., one who is erotic, (2) *anyā*, this is either the married or unmarried heroine (but love for the married one should not be the main sentiment), and (3) *sādhāraṇa strī*, who is the non-marrying type (usually a courtesan). And finally, in accordance with the hero's behaviour towards her she could be one of the following eight types:

1. *Svādhīna-bhartṛkā*, happy one because the husband, already under thumb, is with her;
2. *Vāsakasajjā*, one who is given to make herself up at the time her husband is due to return;
3. *Virahotkanthitā*, one who is unhappy even when her husband, going the right way, is late to return to her;
4. *Khanditā*, one who has hawk's eyes to detect signs of a rival on her own lover and having done so blows up in jealousy;
5. *Kalahāntaritā*, one who angrily repulses her husband who has erred and then repents;
6. *Vipralabdhā*, one who takes insult if the lover fails to keep up the appointment punctually;
7. *Proṣitapriyā*, one whose husband is away on work; and
8. *Abhisārikā*, one who, overcome by passion, herself goes in search of a lover or manages to induce a lover to find her.

Since in Sanskrit plays no heroine appears except in love stories no further types have been given. It is needless to add that every single one of the minor or supporting cast is defined in meticulous details. An ordinary playwright has nothing to worry about 'characterisation' as such while writing the play.

The foregoing was made inevitable in the context of developing the story and constructing it into a drama. As mentioned earlier, the story itself is a number of selected episodes. Naturally, this means that some incidents are brought on the stage and others, though necessary part of the story, are not so important or not so proper. The first is called *vācya,* that which can and should be shown on the stage, and the second, in contrast, is called *sūcya,* lit. that which is suggested (but actually those details of the story which need not or could not or should not be shown on the stage). Though these latter are not shown on the stage, it does not mean that they are not at all relevant to the development of the story. Therefore, when it is said that they should not be shown to the audience the possibility of their being orally conveyed to the audience is there. And Bharata (or *Nāṭyaśāstra*) describes a number of ways in which this could be done.

We have already said that there was no curtain to divide act from act nor was there any such break during the performance. Yet in their written forms (as well as in definition) the division into acts was there. This division was to convey each stage of the story as it was completed. But as the performance was continuous one, it was necessary to fill-up the gaps between one stage and the next. This was done by a number of devices.

There are what are called 'interludes' or scenes that connect one with the other. These interludes tell us what happened (unshown to the audience) and connect it with what is going to be shown next. In these interludes only 'middle' or 'low' characters must participate; in the former case it is *viṣkambhaka* and in the latter *praveśaka*. In case middle and low characters come together in an interlude it is a special kind of *viṣkambhaka* (*miśra*—or mixed it is called). The interludes are always between two acts; but the *viṣkambhaka* in addition can be employed at the beginning of the first act too. This is easy to understand. Even when the story is well-known it would be, sometimes, necessary to start the dramatisation from a particular point onwards in the story and in such cases the summary of the part of the story that is not being shown as well as the episode from which the start is being made have to be conveyed to the audience. It could be done only through a *viṣkambhaka*, or it should be done through 'low' characters.

Apart from these two there are other devices which deserve notice, viz.: (1) *cūlikā*, (2) *aṅkāsya* and (3) *aṅkāvatāra*.

1. *Cūlikā* is the device in which a character, off the stage, introduces the scene, and then enters on the stage and narrates what has passed in the meanwhile and what is to follow.
2. In *aṅkāsya* the character on the stage at the end of the preceding act introduces the beginning of the next act and the exits (the end of an act is usually denoted by the exit of all the characters on the stage).
3. Finally, *aṅkāvatāra* is a device in which the end of the preceding act telescopes, so to say, into the beginning of the next act.

It is not necessary to comment on these nor on a few others in which the characters, not necessarily at the end of an act nor to connect two stages, convey to us, oftentimes, what is supposed to have passed unshown to us. For example, a character may indulge in a soliloquy which is supposed not to be heard by other characters, or an aside or *sotto voce* as it is called.

There is only one thing left out in the context of play-writing and that is the prologue which follows the *pūrvaraṅga* but precedes the beginning of a play. In this prologue which is outside the story, the *sūtradhāra*, or *sthāpaka* as he is called when he comes before the audience, welcomes the audience, usually flatters it (to put it into a proper mood), gives information about the author and the play (here too like a publicity agent he is very complimentary) and explains the context in or the reason for which the play is to be performed. Incidentally, he praises the actors (including himself, of course). In some cases, he goes further by asking *naṭī*, his female counterpart, to sing and/or to dance.

So now we know how play and its performance are to be introduced to the audience and how it is to be constructed as well. The only thing that remains is to see if at the end the critics and the audience feel 'entertained' in the sense in which Bharata used the word *vinoda* (= entertainment).

10

Rasa Theory

It is interesting to note that Bharata, in the *Nāṭyaśāstra,* has not only defined for us characters on the stage but even characters in the auditorium. As we have referred to above more than once, one of the reasons which Bharata advances for evolving his theory and definition of a dramatic representation is his regretful observation that by then these shows had deteriorated into something, *grāmya,* i.e., vulgar. At the same time he always pleads that a dramatic show must be open to all. In effect, these two views would conflict with each other. If a show is open to all, then you cannot insist on its being high-brow and not *grāmya*; if likewise, the tone of a show is to be raised to a cultured level, you would feel compelled to choose your audience. You cannot both have your cake and eat it, as the proverb goes. For his own days, Bharata seems to have cleverly resolved this conflict. He is in favour of selecting a story that is very well-known and he is also inclined, to judge from the details of his rules for a good drama, towards love-stories. Now these two conditions, a well-known story and a love-story are in themselves sufficient to attract an audience whose education and intelligence would not qualify for things more subtle; and then he has his own theories of *sandhis* and *rasa* and enlightenment which could tempt a high-brow audience. It is this cleverness of Bharata which Kālidāsa indirectly extols in his plays (in one of which there is also a reference to Bharata and a production by him) by saying that "drama is a type of entertainment that would capture the hearts of people of different tastes".

The *sūtradhāra* of a play, according to Bharata, praises (even flatters) the audience in the prologue. The qualities imagined in the audience for which it is flattered are just the qualities which Bharata prescribes for an audience. In the *Nāṭyaśāstra,* in chapter XXVII (51 ff), the qualities of an audience are described thus:

> A spectator is one who has no obvious faults, who is attached to drama, whose senses are not liable to distraction, who is clever in guessing (putting two and two together), who can enjoy (others') joy and sympathise with (others') sorrows, who suffers with those who suffer and who has all these nine qualities in himself.

A more common sense point of view of and a more modest expectation from an audience cannot be easily found. Bharata does not encourage, e.g., a drunken man (obvious fault), or one who comes for the sake of company (not attached to drama) or one who is easily diverted by 'other' attractions in the auditorium (liable to distraction) or one who has no imaginative power of his own. In other words, a spectator should be one who could easily lose himself in the characters on the stage, their joys and sorrows.

When an individual spectator is expected to be such a man of refined and transparent sensibilities, it is easy to guess how strict and exacting Bharata could be regarding the qualities of a critic; a critic should further be one of an open-mind (*madhyastha*), one who knows about music and dance, one who is well-informed about the four kinds of acting and one who has good acquaintance with the different dialects and customs.

An audience must be such as could appreciate the artistic point of a dramatic show. What is meant by such an appreciation?

In answer to this question, Bharata has evolved *rasa* (theory). Though the *rasa* theory is more associated with poetry, it originated first in relation to drama only and Bharata is credited with its origin. A later writer called Rudraṭa (AD 850) has actually said that within his limited abilities he was explaining the *rasa* theory as applied to poetry though "by Bharata and others it was evolved mainly in relation to drama". The appeal of the *rasa* theory and its aptness to describe appreciation has been extolled by all later writers. Dhanañjaya, the author of the treatise called *Daśarūpaka* (dealing with dramaturgy) has this to say of *rasa*:

> Anything, be it beautiful or ugly, dignified or despicable, or dreadful or of pleasing appearance, deep or deformed, object or non-object, whatever it be it, could be turned into *rasa* by poet's imaginative power (IV, 85).

In chapters VI and VII of the *Nāṭyaśāstra*, Bharata explains *rasa* and *bhāva*. The sages, sitting around Bharata, ask him the following questions: (1) What is that called *rasa* by experts in dramaturgy? (2) What is a *bhāva* and why is it called so? (3) What is a *saṁgraha*? a *kārikā*? and *nirukta*? The very first question is about *rasa*. "We shall explain first about *rasa*" says Bharata. Why first? Because, "without *rasa*, no purpose is fulfilled".

The two chapters, however, seem to have been interfered with by many other writers. There are too many repetitive passages; there are passages that conflict with or contradict other passages, references to and quotations from others are more here than in any other chapters; and, the prose passages, not always explanatory, seem to have been written in a later style. As a matter of fact, it seems as if the discussion of *rasa* was an independent text and like the chapters on music and dancing these two chapters were edited and collected in the *Nāṭyaśāstra* itself. In chapter VI in the opening 32 verses the author summarises *rasas, bhāvas, abhinaya, vṛttis,* etc., in almost the same order in which the subjects are discussed in this and the following chapters. These 32 verses are like the chapter of contents, as we see in the *Mahābhārata* (e.g., the chapter called *yadāśrauṣam*).

The main idea of *rasa* and of the *bhāva,* however, can be gleaned with little difficulty.

1. 'The name *rasa* is applied because this is something which can be relished like the taste of food.' (chapter VI.)
2. 'The feeling (*bhāva*) that is intended by the poet is conveyed by words, bodily gestures and acting, etc. So these latter are called *bhāvas.*' (VII, 2.)

In explaining the idea of *rasa,* an example is given of a meal in which the menu consists of dishes of different tastes like hot, sweet, pungent, etc.; while each dish is eaten, each different taste is being enjoyed, and the diner, while eating, not only shows by his face or his eyes, etc., but by some actual remarks or exclamations his appreciation of each different taste. After the meal is over if he says "it was real good, delicious food, I have enjoyed it", what does he mean? Is he referring to each and every taste separately of the various dishes? Or is there a combined taste so to say? What is this general feeling of satisfaction which he expresses with reference to the entire meal? And what does he precisely mean by saying he has enjoyed the meal? By his facial expressions and exclamations we could understand his enjoyment of the different tastes individually. Now are there any other signs which could convey this general satisfaction he mentions? For the sake of the example, we may recall one of our many friends of demonstrative habits. The picture of this friend is somewhat like this: he is enjoying the different tastes as is quite obvious from his exclamations and reactions to each taste. Then the meal is over; he sits in a relaxing position; he closes his eyes, silently smacks his lips and then sits for a few seconds with a smile on his lip but like one who is asleep. Then as if suddenly waking up and recalling something he says, "I have enjoyed the meal!" In this analysis, the moments preceding to his sudden "waking" up are the moments of *rasa*; just before that when he relaxes and smacks his lips he has got into a mood which could be called the *sthāyī bhāva*. So, the *āsvāda*, i.e., the relishing of the *rasa*, i.e., the feeling of complete satisfaction is conveyed to us during those few moments when, apparently, he is doing nothing and saying nothing.

Later writers, particularly his admirers and commentators, have tried to make this idea as abstruse as possible; but, as it is explained in the *Nāṭyaśāstra*, it is a simple, straightforward, common sense point of view. The example of food and its relish emphasises this. *Rasa*, as Bharata explains, is the final state of relish or satisfaction but that state follows many others, as we have seen with various different tastes. These different tastes with their reactions, etc., and preceding the ultimate satisfaction, are called as *bhāvas* and Bharata says that *rasa* is the result of and from the *bhāvas* and not *vice versa* as some believe. This *bhāva* is nothing but what expresses a reaction, be it by bodily gestures or by words. The conception of *bhāva* too is analysed by Bharata and in doing so he uses four words, viz., *vibhāva, anubhāva, vyabhicāribhāva* and finally *sthāyībhāva.*

The meanings of these words may be made clear by an example. Suppose, *A* challenges *B* or quarrels with *B* or annoys him for some thing. In that case, *B* will get angry. That anger shows itself through his (*B*'s) distended nostrils, or his biting lips or trembling, etc. And then *B* in his anger would raise his hand to hit *A* or shout in anger and so on. In this example, we notice three different processes: (1) *A* challenging or quarrelling or annoying *B*; (2) *B*'s appearance with red eyes or distended nostrils or biting his lips, etc.; and (3) *B* raising his hand to strike or tremble with rage or shout at *A*. Considering the entire process from *B*'s point of view we can say that factor (1) is the cause for *B*'s subsequent behaviour. Now *B* has got angry but the anger is still unexploded. We can say this because of factor (2) in which the red eyes or distended nostrils or the biting of lips is the external sign of the anger inside. But how did the signs appear? Did *B* intentionally show them? No. We know from experience that such things are the immediate involuntary reactions to surroundings. They are beyond our control. When we cut our fingers our mind may be trained enough not to feel the hurt or the pain; but the body naturally bleeds. Bleeding is the automatic reaction of the body (or can we say of the mind conditioned by millions and millions of years?) to the hurt? Red eyes, etc., are like that in the case of an angry man. Factor (1) which is a cause but an external one is called the *vibhāva* and factor (2) which is the immediate and involuntary reaction is called the *anubhāva.* Now that *B* has all the signs of an angry man he then acts, i.e., behaves as an angry man is supposed to behave. (3) He raises his hand to strike *A,* he begins to tremble (because he is trying to control what is beyond him to control) and he also begins to shout. This third factor is the wilful, deliberate or conscious reaction of *B* as against the involuntary reaction in (2). So, in contrast to the latter the conscious or voluntary reaction is called the *vyabhicārībhāva*. Finally, there is a total effect of his reaction and behaviour on himself to the extent that he forgets himself, when his entire individuality takes, so to say, a different appearance and even when all the involuntary and voluntary reactions are not perceptible, there is a short interval during which one could clearly perceive him as an angry man. This interval is distinguished as a *sthāyībhāva*. It is the *sthāyībhāva* that constitutes the *rasa*. The author of the *Nāṭyaśāstra* (chapter VII prose passage following verse 7) gives a number of examples and says finally that the *sthāyībhāvas* are like the master, the other three *bhāvas* are its servants and though all together go to make up the *rasa* one can say the *sthāyībhāvaṣ* are the *rasa* since they alone dominate among the four.

From the foregoing analysis, one can understand better Bharata's rules about acting. We have seen earlier a detailed description of the distinction between different types of heroes and heroines. Each type is expected to act the *anubhāvas* and the *vyabhicārībhāvas*. As a matter of fact the entire chapters (XXII, XXV, 41ff) concerned with this classification deal with acting of these two *bhāvas*. Later books on the subject go to the length of saying that *sāttvika* or *sāmānya abhinaya* is nothing but the acting of the *anubhāva* and the *vyabhicārībhāva*.

The *Nāṭyaśāstra* recognises eight *sthāyībhāvas*:

1. *Rati* or Love:
   - (a) *Vibhāva*: stimulus would be season, flower, ornaments or anything beautiful or desirable.
   - (b) *Anubhāva*: or involuntary reaction: looking sideways, coy glance, sweet words, etc.

(c) *Vyabhicāribhāva*: lassitude, suspicion, jealousy, etc.

2. *Hāsya* or humour:
   (a) *Vibhāva*: peculiarity of dress or speech, etc.
   (b) *Anubhāva*: spouting, mimicking, etc.
   (c) *Vyabhicāribhāva*: smile, snicker, laughter, guffow, etc.
3. *Karuṇā* or compassion:
   (a) *Vibhāva*: loss, death, calamity, etc.
   (b) *Anubhāva*: tears, fainting, lamentations, etc.
   (c) *Vyabhicāribhāva*: sorrow, trembling, fear, etc.
4. *Rudra* or horror:
   (a) *Vibhāva*: anger, violence, treachery, etc.
   (b) *Anubhāva*: red eyes, rubbing hands, biting lips, etc.
   (c) *Vyabhicāribhāva*: sweating, excitement, impatience, etc.
5. *Vīra* or heroic:
   (a) *Vibhāva*: determination, strength, bravery, etc.
   (b) *Anubhāva*: courage, generosity, etc.
   (c) *Vyabhicāribhāva*: decision, arrogance, etc.
6. *Bhayāṇaka* or fear:
   (a) *Vibhāva*: frightful things, lonely sights, etc.
   (b) *Anubhāva*: trembling, pallor, loosing voice, etc.
   (c) *Vyabhicāribhāva*: fainting, hurrying, standing rooted, etc.
7. *Bībhatsa* or awesome:
   (a) *Vibhāva*: bad news, loud lamentations, etc.
   (b) *Anubhāva*: repulsion, spitting, turning up nose, etc.
   (c) *Vyabhicāribhāva*: fainting, illness, death, etc.
8. *Adbhuta* or wonder:
   (a) *Vibhāva*: Seeing unusual things; achieving the desired, magic, etc.

(b) *Anubhāva*: wide or staring eyes, thrill, exclamations, etc.

(c) *Vyabhicārībhāva*: standing stunned, over-joy, etc.

It may be noted that as these various *bhāvas* are listed (chapters VI-VII), sometimes we find a confusion or a conflict in distinguishing one reaction from the other. But as these two chapters seem to have suffered worse manhandling one need not feel uncertain about the basic general idea. Secondly, though in some cases the *vyabhicārībhāva* seem to be identical, it must be noted that as individual reactions these vary from person to person. But *anubhāva* being natural or immediate reactions would be common to larger numbers. *Vyabhicārībhāvas* are also called *saṁcārībhāvas* because they change from person to person.

Lastly, there is one more *rasa* called *śānta* or content or peace which was recognised later. We are not sure if it was recognised by Bharata; most probably it was not, because Bharata's very conception of *rasa* led to content. But those who recognised it did so because it was a different kind of content, viz., final bliss or *mokṣa*. That is why the *vibhāva* for this *rasa* is knowledge or truth, detachment or purity of intent, etc., *anubhāva* is self-control, meditation, universal sympathy and the like; while, the *vyabhicārībhāva* is purity, firmness, thrill, etc.

But in a drama only the first eight *rasas* have a place and are recognised. The success of a performance is determined by the extent of the audience relishing the particular *rasa* of the play. It has been said that drama is meant for persons of different tastes. For this reason, Bharata desires more than one *rasa*; the many the merrier so to say, in a play. But always only one *rasa* must be predominant and other subordinate to it.

11

Conclusion

The *Nāṭyaśāstra,* as it is available, deals not only with drama but with music and dances as well. As a matter of fact in some editions (or MSS), at the end of the last (XXXVII) chapter, the colophon at the end says that the book is finished and then the name of the book is given as *Nandī Bharata Saṅgīta-pustakam*—the book on music by Nandī Bharata! But in spite of all such tempering and confusion, here and there one finds facts or fancies from which some truth could be gleaned.

Chapter XXXVI is called the chapter "on the curse on actors". Here, the sages who have been listening to Bharata "intently" decide to ask a question which they had not asked till now lest they disturbed Bharata. You have told us that drama is the story of the world. Now, for example, of which world is the story in the *pūrvaraṅga*? Secondly, how did drama drop down from Heavenly World? And, thirdly, how did it happen that your descendants (i.e., actors) were cursed?

Bharata listened to them and decided to reveal the secret (verse 10). "Now, about *pūrvaraṅga,* I have already told you that it was there (not as part of any story) but to ward off obstacle...and because of the music and the flattery, the gods were extremely pleased with it.... In the course of time, however, it so happened that the artists, in vulgar taste, began lampooning the sages who consequently got angry and cursed the artists to a low and vulgar life. The gods coming to know of it felt very sorry and feared that drama would perish.... The sages assured them that that would not happen but otherwise the curse would be effective.... Then my sons turned on me and said that it was because of me that they slipped into this calamity.... 'Because of your drama we are now condemned to be śūdras,' they complained. But I pacified them and told them that any way it was not their end and they should see that drama also did not come to its end. Remember that just as Brahmā gave it to me, we should pass it on to our disciples."

Thus the condemned actors were cursed to be born as śūdras on the earth (till now Bharata had his theatre in the world of gods only) and, on Bharata's advice, brought with them drama as well. That, however, was not the end of the story.

Time passed. A mortal king called Nahuṣa won the kingdom of gods by his valour and cleverness and came to rule it. One day he expressed a desire to see a dramatic performance. While on earth he had thoroughly enjoyed drama but later on (for want of actresses) when the harem was destroyed drama too was destroyed. But now in the heavenly world there were *apsaras* women, so Nahuṣa desired a performance.

But the gods told him that it was not a practicable idea since *apsaras*—ladies belong to the heavenly world—could not mix with the male actors who belong to the mortal world. Then Nahuṣa appealed to Bharata who said that king's command must be carried out and for that purpose, he would see that the duration of the curse ended.

He saw to it too.

Like the Indian drama, its story too has a happy ending.

Index